HR – The Business Partner

HR – The Business Partner: Shaping a New Direction

Barbara Kenton and Jane Yarnall

ELSEVIER
BUTTERWORTH
HEINEMANN

AMSTERDAM • BOSTON • HEIDELBERG • LONDON • NEW YORK • OXFORD
PARIS • SAN DIEGO • SAN FRANCISCO • SINGAPORE • SYDNEY • TOKYO

Elsevier Butterworth-Heinemann
Linacre House, Jordan Hill, Oxford OX2 8DP
30 Corporate Drive, Burlington, MA 01803

First published 2005
Reprinted 2006

British Library Cataloguing in Publication Data
A catalogue record for this book is available from the British Library

Library of Congress Cataloguing in Publication Data
A catalogue record for this book is available from the Library of Congress

ISBN 0 7506 6454 1

For information on all Elsevier Butterworth-Heinemann
publications visit our website at www.bh.com

Working together to grow
libraries in developing countries

www.elsevier.com | www.bookaid.org | www.sabre.org

ELSEVIER   BOOK AID   Sabre Foundation
             International

Typeset by Integra Software Services Pvt. Ltd., Pondicherry, India
www.integra-india.com
Printed and bound in Great Britain

Contents

List of Figures

List of Tables

Foreword

Contemporary organisations face constant pressure to enhance levels of service and productivity whilst also improving levels of cost efficiency. The volatility of external environment and the rapid pace of technological change increasingly demand innovative means of improving business performance and securing competitive advantage. Human resources are increasingly recognised as the prime source of competitive advantage and the need for effective people management is therefore more important than ever before. The responsibility for effective people management is shared between senior managers, HR professionals and line managers but the challenges facing today's organisations provide an ideal opportunity for the HR function to demonstrate its ability to contribute to organisational performance at a strategic level. To take advantage of this opportunity it is necessary to not only recognise the changes that are required but also identify the steps to ensure that they can be implemented effectively.

Whilst much has been written about strategic human resource management and its contribution to organisational performance, real-life examples of what works and what doesn't remain thin on the ground. We recognise that HR professionals and senior managers alike face a sometimes overwhelming pressure to follow trends or apply quick-fixes to a wide range of people management challenges and it can be difficult to get impartial advice about what to change and how to change it in order to create lasting results. We have therefore developed this series to bridge the gap between theory and implementation by providing workable solutions to complex people management issues and by sharing organisational experiences. The books within this series draw on live examples of strategic HR in practice and offer practical insights, tools and frameworks that will help to transform the individual and functional delivery of HR within a variety of organisational contexts.

The authors of this fascinating book, Barbara Kenton and Jane Yarnall, draw on their insights gained from working as consultants with HR teams throughout the UK, their career experience in HR and management development roles, as well as their detailed research to show what being an HR Business Partner means in practice. They look at some of the typical challenges of the role and at what can be done to address them. They include a number of case studies demonstrating leading practice in this rapidly evolving area. The authors provide practical insights into how to develop the skills and confidence required to really make a difference in Business Partner roles. While much of the authors' focus is on Business Partner roles in Human Resources, the same principles apply in large measure to other value-added specialist roles.

Acting as Business Partner

Dave Ulrich defines one of the key domains of strategic HR as being 'Business Partner' with line management. The authors show how being a Business Partner means working in tandem with the business, focusing on the big 'people', 'culture', 'change' and 'capability' issues as well as helping find positive solutions in the here and now. The distinction can be drawn between being reactive and being strategically responsive – both leading and following. At senior levels, really strategic Business Partners are proactive – they influence those who make the business strategies, working alongside or as part of the business planning team to develop strategies together. Business Partners need a good understanding of the business and its changing context; they need to be clear about the organisation's goals, needs, values; aware of gaps in culture and capability; to be able to translate business goals into operational strategies. They need to be able to influence decision-makers. Good negotiation and interpersonal skills, as well as resilience, may be required.

HR Business Partners are often described as 'knowledge rich' but poor in application. Being strategic alone is not enough. Chief Executives want HR professionals to be able to translate the organisational issues into business language, and vice versa. They need HR Business Partners to help them understand what must be done with regard to people if business strategies are to be achieved. If as an HR

Business Partner you are able to say: 'I'm here to help you as CEO and I think I can get a better brand', you need to be able to deliver the kind of cultural shifts which will produce the business results. CEOs do not want an over-engineered appraisal system delivered late. They are looking for a jargon-free and pragmatic approach to creating an organisation which delivers results in the here and now, as well as in the future.

This means that HR professionals at all levels need to be able to sense the issues which count, and have the confidence to relay some potentially tough messages to management about what needs to be done. This is the quality Dave Ulrich calls 'HR with attitude'. CEOs also need HR to be experts in process skills, able to influence and win support and commitment within the organisation.

Personal Credibility

Personal credibility is key. For Business Partners credibility is usually gained through high-quality delivery of programmes and initiatives which made a difference to line management and the business, such as helping to reduce stress in the workplace, getting to the root cause of problems rather than inventing a new 'sticking plaster' process. Business Partners need to be able to act as internal consultants, working with line managers in problem-solving ways, concentrating on reality, demonstrating business acumen and ensuring that HR and business goals are one and the same. They need to be externally focused, in touch with current thinking, having extensive networks and able to apply insights gained in a practical way. They need to be able to work effectively with colleagues in shared services and centres of excellence, ensuring the highest-quality client delivery.

Change Management

Business Partners need to be able to manage culture change. Most organisations see the need at some stage to develop new ways of working and to change old patterns of behaviour. HR Business Partners should ideally be catalysts for change, working alongside line management to define the desired culture and find ways of changing attitudes and behaviours, especially those of people in leadership positions.

They need to be able to facilitate change, deal constructively with conflict and manage the politics of the situation. They require a good range of change process skills and approaches, including programme management and planning.

Developing the ability to see what needs to be changed may simply be a matter of making time to think – not easy in the daily grind of meetings and tasks. Bringing about change requires being prepared to challenge the status quo. Knowing what needs to be done requires focus, working collaboratively with Business Partners, using your own understanding and intuition to make good decisions and being able to bring others with you. This involves being able to influence others and challenge constructively.

How Can This Book Help?

Sometimes there is no substitute for simply having a go, but it helps if you have built up support for your ideas first. The good news is that many of the skills required for today's more complex HR roles can be learnt off the job too. Barbara Kenton and Jane Yarnall have here provided a practical guide for people embarking on Business Partner roles for the first time, as well as a useful touchstone for experienced Business Partners from any discipline who wish to refocus their practice.

Julie Beardwell
Principal Lecturer in Human Resource Management
De Montfort University

Linda Holbeche
Director of Research
Roffey Park Institute

Acknowledgements

There are so many people who have contributed to this book either overtly or indirectly that sadly it is impossible to give credit to them all.

We are particularly grateful to the organisations and people working as Business Partners who contributed their time and energy in talking to us about the research. We also want to acknowledge the many other authors whose work we have drawn on to bring you this book. They have helped stretch our thinking and widened the circle of knowledge by their generosity in allowing us to use their work here.

In addition, we would like to thank our colleagues, in particular Linda Holbeche who has supported our writing and provided inspiration through her own work; Diane Moody and other colleagues at Roffey Park Institute who continually challenge our thinking and provide their own unique perspective on topics around organisational and people development; John Gilkes, the Chief Executive at Roffey Park, who again has supported our work; and the clients who have provided case studies for this book.

We would also like to add a special thanks to Debbie Beaney for formatting the book so that it was in great shape to go to the publishers, and Clive Ruffle, in the Learning Resources Centre (LRC) at Roffey Park, for he and his colleagues in the LRC have really helped us to check out references and copyright issues. Thanks must also go to Francesca Ford and Ailsa Marks at Elsevier publishing for making this possible.

Finally, we would like to thank our partners for supporting us along the way and providing both encouragement and tolerance at just the right times.

1

Introduction

You do not need to navigate a company to a pre-defined destination, you take steps – one at a time into an unknowable future. There are not paths, no roads ahead of us. In the final analysis, it is the walking that beats the path – it is not the path that makes the walk.

Poet Machada in the 5th Discipline – Peter Senge, 1990

At the time of writing this book, one job title that seemed to be on the increase for people working at a strategic level within organisations and within a broadly HR role seemed to be that of 'Business Partner'. For this reason, and based on our experiences of working with people inside organisations with the specific challenge of implementing change, we decided to write this book.

In this chapter, we examine the history of the role of the Business Partner and the drivers for the changing role of HR. We also look at what it means to be a Business Partner in broad terms and how this differs from the role of both the internal and the external consultant.

If we look at the title in more detail – what do the terms 'Business' and 'Partner' imply? – 'Business' implies a level of strategic intervention which goes beyond the individual. This differentiates an historic role of HR as being just about people and working at an operational level. It also implies that those in the role will have a good understanding of the nature of the business and therefore be in a good position to advise others in this respect. 'Business' also conjures up a level of professionalism and credibility, a matter of factness, which sets apart people in this role from the more traditional and operational HR roles.

Therefore, the role of the Business Partner includes having a good understanding of strategy and what it means to be working more strategically. The role of the Business Partner is to turn strategy into action – to make it happen in reality.

'Partner' and what this title conjures up is something very different. 'Partnership' implies working alongside, equal responsibility and shared skills and expertise, and supporting clients within the business rather than coming from an expert perspective. Put these two together and you get an idea of the role of the Business Partner – someone who maintains a strong connection with employees and the operational side of the business while focusing on strategic goals and influencing through others.

A Little of the History of HR

'Human Resources' still seems a strange title for anything related to people and although we have used it in our book title in recognition of the reality that it is still widely used in business, it seems old-fashioned and somewhat out of date. It conjures up a function which views human beings as innate objects to be factored into an equation. Perhaps unsurprising then is that people in the role of HR have not always been viewed that favourably. There is a sense of people being thought of as commodities to be done unto rather than as co-creators of the organisation; its culture and future. Perhaps also due to the power of the HR role, particularly in areas such as recruitment, rewards, performance management and downsizing, it has been viewed with mixed feelings.

Much has now been written about the evolving role of HR and the shift from a more transactional to strategic or transformational role. Here, we summarise the trends rather than go into them in great detail for the purpose of putting the other chapters into context.

Many authors have compared the traditional role of HR with an emerging need for a more strategic function. The model shown in Table 1.1 highlights some of the comparators between the transactional and the strategic functions.

Traditionally, the role of HR has included a fair percentage of administrative work, which in many organisations has now been outsourced, substituted for advanced IT programmes or in some way re-organised within the overall structure of HR. The purpose of these moves has been

Table 1.1 HR roles compared: Transactional vs Strategic

Role of the HR professional	Transactional approach	Strategic approach
Areas of interest	Recruiting, training, pay, work relations	Strategy and culture of the organisation and policy
View of the organisation	Micro	Macro
Client	Employees	Managers and the organisation as a whole
Status in the organisation	Rather weak	Rather strong
Educational requirements	Specialist in human resource management	General HR education with management experience or general manager with HR experience
Time range for activities	Short range	Medium- to long-term range
Business based on	Transactions	Change/transformations

(M. Green, Public Personnel Management, Spring 2002)

to create a more responsive client-centred service which is proactive in its approach to developing the business. In theory, these changes should also create more space for HR professionals to work at a strategic level within the organisation. So rather than being driven by a need within HR for greater power (although this undoubtedly is a spin-off), the changes are needed to keep apace with the fast pace of organisational life and demands now placed on organisations.

These include legislative changes (e.g. equal opportunities legislation, Government modernisation agenda), financial changes, increases in mergers and partnerships across organisations, shifts in employee expectations and needs, and increased opportunities from advanced IT capabilities.

However, the level of development and culture of the organisation is a key factor if HR is to successfully move from a more transactional role to something more strategic. This is a challenge, to say the least, where HR operates as a function distinct and separate from initiatives aimed at people and organisational development (OD or HRD). If the growth and placement of HR does not sit alongside our understanding of organisational development, we are bound to find frustrations and challenges.

Models of the shifting HR role also need to take account of models of organisational development. For example, Harung and Reiber (1995) highlight some useful descriptions of organisational development, which reflect the level of maturity of an organisation.

Reactive	→	Proactive and preventive
Partial perspective	→	Holistic overview
Command and control	→	Collaboration and empowerment
Short-term perspective	→	Long-term perspective
Task-oriented	→	People-oriented
Ambivalent to feedback	→	Welcoming feedback
Resistance to change	→	Innovation and entrepreneurship
Conventional	→	Pathfinding
Significant component of struggle	→	Joyful self-expression and dynamism
Stereotype	→	Plays many roles successfully
First-order learning	→	Second-order learning (learning to learn)
Efficiency (doing things right)	→	Effectiveness (doing right things)
'Win–lose'	→	Towards 'win'

Reproduced from Harung and Reiber (1995) with permission from Emerald Group Publishing Ltd

Harung and Reiber point out that in the earlier stages of development an organisation might only demonstrate the features shown on the left-hand side of the diagram, while organisations in more advanced stages of development would more likely demonstrate those on both sides.

In our experience, when significant change is happening in organisations, responses to change on both an individual and an organisational level can vary between reactive (left-hand side) and proactive or creative (right-hand side).

Senior managers increasingly need input at a strategic level from those with knowledge in HR to help them understand the impact of changes on the organisation and how to make best use of the people employed to make the business a success. Part of the role of the strategic

Business Partner is to help the organisation make the necessary shifts and take the organisation to where it needs to be.

It would be remiss of us to omit the work of David Ulrich in this chapter as he has long championed the role of HR as strategic Business Partner, linking it to a business imperative for a more proactive approach from HR with less reliance on operational expertise.

The axes in David Ulrich's (1997) model show how HR practitioners can be anywhere between having a day-to-day or operational focus and being more strategic and future focused and having a focus on HR processes and systems or people (Figure 1.1). Ulrich describes the four roles as follows:

1. *Strategic partner* – helps to successfully execute business strategy and meet customer needs
2. *Administrative experts* – constantly improve organisational efficiency by re-engineering the HR function and other work processes
3. *Employee champions* – maximise employee commitment and competence
4. *Change agents* – deliver organisational transformation and culture change.

Clearly the aspirational role of the Business Partner would seem to be aimed at delivering strategic objectives in line with all of the above.

Figure 1.1 Ulrich's matrix

Most would agree that to achieve and maintain this high level of strategic intervention is challenging. Those truly skilled in these areas can command a high salary and with that goes a high expectation of what they can deliver. Certainly the role has become more complex and in our discussions with HR practitioners it would seem that people are providing a whole host of services without very neat boundaries or role distinction.

What then is a Business Partner?

Roffey Park research, carried out in 1999 in conjunction with *Personnel Today*, identified from 200 practitioners that 61 per cent of respondents still felt HR was too reactive and 60 per cent felt HR spent too much time on trivial matters, despite 71 per cent saying that personnel had been fully or partly devolved to the line. Whilst this research was done several years ago, in our experience and research, the vision of strategic Business Partnering is some way off being fully realised.

A Business Partner, according to Linda Holbeche, Director of Research at Roffey Park Institute, is someone who:

> *Works alongside senior managers, providing the link between business and organisational strategies, providing support and challenge to the senior team and developing credible initiatives in a setting of ongoing cost reduction.*
>
> (Holbeche, 1999)

What would a Business Partner be doing that someone in a more traditional HR role might not? And how would we notice?

For one thing the Business Partner would have a seat at the Executive table and be seen to be an equal partner in making strategic decisions about the business. They would be making contributions to organisational design, strategy development and planning and organisational change. There would be substantially less time spent on a maintenance role – for example, hands-on recruitment, maintaining services and records, and auditing.

Some of the key functions of the Business Partner are shown below:

- Strategic planning
- Organisational development and design
- Improving organisational productivity and quality
- Facilitating mergers, acquisitions and partnerships
- Scanning the environment for new products/potential new partnerships
- Recruitment and selection – strategy rather than implementation
- Employee development – training/education; management development; performance appraisal; career planning; competency/talent assessment – again strategy and advice on these areas rather than carrying out the strategy
- Compensation and benefits – reward and recognition initiatives; retirement programmes; redundancy programmes
- Management of HR information systems
- Overseeing Trade Union negotiations
- Responsibility for legal and regulatory requirements – equal opportunities policy and practice; employee record keeping.

The difference between an operational HR role and a strategic Business Partner goes beyond changing job descriptions to looking more carefully at the skills required and the capacity for individuals to influence change at a strategic level.

> *the consensus seems to be that change is required both in the skills of individuals in the HR function and the way the HR function is organised and carries out its activities.*
>
> (Lawler and Mohrman, 2003)

How Does the Business Partner Role Compare to that of a Consultant?

In this introduction, we wanted to pay some attention to the role of the consultant and highlight similarities and differences between the roles of Business Partner, internal and external consultants. In our view, the consultancy skills set is a key area for Business Partners to develop and we devote a chapter to this later in the book.

Much has been written about the purpose and nature of the consultant role (Block, 1981; Cockman et al., 1992; Lippit and Lippit, 1986). The consultant role is typically defined through its separation from the system it serves; the consultant holds neither line responsibility nor budget, though may often have status and recognition.

> *A person in a position to have some influence over an individual, group or organisation, but who has no direct power to make changes or implement programmes.*
>
> (Block, 1981)

Given their externality to the client system and lack of formal power to impose change, the most the consultant can hope for is to influence the client through credibility, expertise, skills, knowledge and understanding to change something. They do this through their interventions, coming into the client system and leaving once the client has been helped.

Whilst most writing on consultancy draws upon the external consultant as an example, writers accept that there are particular issues faced by consultants operating from within. It is recognised that Internal Consultants possess many of the skills deployed by their external counterparts (Armstrong, 1992; Duncan and Nixon, 1999; Laabs, 1997). They have the additional advantage of knowing the business – its systems, language and culture from the inside. However the Internal Consultant works within a complex contractual environment where reporting lines may be the same as that of their client. They will typically not hold budgetary or other powers to enforce change and may be perceived as agents of a broader corporate agenda rather than true client helpers. As Armstrong (1992) states:

> *Internal consultants may have just as much expertise, although as employees it may be more difficult for them to be – or to be seen to be – as independent as those from outside the organisation. They have to demonstrate that they are able to deliver truly objective advice.*

If the role of the Internal Consultant is to facilitate change, then particular challenges exist over and above those facing consultants from outside. The skills and attributes they bring to the role are often overlooked when Line Managers look for support to achieve change, so Internal Consultants can find themselves busy with mundane operational tasks whilst external consultants get the more challenging, strategic projects. This sidelining is a function of many factors: the credibility of the consultants themselves, their ability to market their offerings, the micropolitical landscape, and status and value issues connected to consultancy use.

Typically the Internal Consultant is drawn from one of the teams of professional service providers such as HR, IT or finance where there is a history of supporting internal customers with specific problems.

Writers agree (Armstrong, 1992; Duncan and Nixon, 1999; Laabs, 1997) that the Internal Consultant's role is to lead and influence change through supporting clients to learn and apply new skills. In this sense, there is a tension in the Internal Consultant's role; how to help the client, where the best help that can be given may not be aligned to the organisation's agenda.

Block (2001) recognises these tensions, 'Because you work for the same organisation, line managers can see you as being captured by the same forces and madness that impinge on them. Thus they may be a little slower to trust you and recognise that you have something special to offer them.'

Therefore a set of core skills are required to ensure success. Key to these, according to Roffey Park's Management Agenda (McCartney and Holbeche, 2003), are: facilitating change, relationship building, active listening skills and understanding the nature of change.

The main differentiating factors between internal and external consultants are summarised in Table 1.2.

Table 1.2 Internal/External Consultants: Key differences in role

External	Internal
Credibility through brand status and previous experience	Credibility through history of interactions within the business
Broad business perspective – bringing new ideas	Deep organisational perspective
Limited organisation-specific knowledge, possibly at content level only – 'Not made here'	Understands its culture, language and deeper symbolic actions
Perceived as objective	Perceived as an organisational 'agent'
Special	The same
Low investment in final success	High investment in final success
Meets client's agenda	Meets corporate agenda – which may not be client's
Needs time to understand the people – may misinterpret actions and interpersonal dynamics	Knows the people, but may have preconceptions
'On the clock' – timed, expensive, rare and rationed	Free, accessible, and available

There are many similarities between the list on the right-hand side and the Business Partner role. The topic of whose agenda you are meeting is discussed in more detail throughout the book.

Challenges and tensions

In Kenton and Moody's research (2003) Internal Consultants were asked what they felt were the biggest challenges facing them as Internal Consultants, by far the most frequently mentioned were:

- Lack of understanding of the role within the business
- Lack of trust
- Lack of senior management support
- Lack of power to action projects/proposals.

These issues also link to our research and discussions around challenges for those in the role of Business Partner.

So although the definitions of Internal Consultant may seem fairly clear, what this means in behavioural terms is not so straightforward. We found many Internal Consultants very unclear about the boundaries of their role – particularly in the early stages of setting up a service. This has led to role ambiguity on the part of both the consultant and their internal clients.

We have taken the view that there will be a number of people working inside the organisation, who may be called Business Partner or HR Advisor, Change Agent, Internal Consultant or variations on these themes. Whilst the roles may differ in the level of authority and specific remit, there will be some common challenges to all. This book aims to provide useful advice and considerations for anyone in an internal consultancy position.

Throughout the book we use the terms 'Business Partner' and 'Internal Consultant' intermittently as in our view the Business Partner also needs to be an Internal Consultant, although depending on definitions the Internal Consultant will not necessarily need to be a Business Partner! We also use the terms 'client', 'sponsor' and 'stakeholders' and these terms are explored in more detail in Part 1.

Background to Our Research Approach and Framework for this Book

Our research for the book was carried out in the following ways:

- Informal interviews on the telephone and in person with HR practitioners
- Gathering stories over a number of years from consultancy programmes including the Roffey Park residential programme (Consultancy skills for Organisational Change)
- Data from Roffey Park's Management Agenda
- Desk research – reading and research from books and articles on consultancy, HR practice, OD and change
- Questionnaires and interviews towards 'The Role of the Internal Consultant' by Barbara Kenton and Diane Moody
- Ongoing discussions with colleagues working in a similar field.

Much of the research was emergent and our perceptions have changed during the course of writing this book. No doubt by the time it is published, ours and others' thinking will have moved on further still; however, we believe the nature of the book will mean it still provides valuable pointers for HR practitioners.

Some of the assumptions which underpin this work are:

- Those in the role of Business Partner or working towards this are in challenging and demanding roles
- Many people in HR working in this way are already highly skilled
- People who want to work more strategically within the business could do with some help
- Learning comes through sharing ideas and experiences
- Learning can come through challenge and success
- Noticing what works well is as helpful as noticing what does not
- It helps to look outside our own organisation at practice elsewhere to see what might work for our own organisations
- The more Business Partners can understand the whole system the more effective they are likely to be.

We have adapted the model by Harung and Reiber (1995), described earlier in this chapter, to provide a framework which incorporates some of the characteristics of a mature organisation to reflect the strategic role of the Business Partner. You may want to compare this with any existing competency frameworks you have in place or use it to define new ones.

We should stress that this includes generic behaviours, more aligned to the *process* of Business Partnering. Specific behaviours for example around organisational design might need to be added in, although we would warn against making the list too long or complex.

Sections in this book focus on key areas as follows:

- Section 1 – Delivering to the business
- Section 2 – Working alongside managers, Self-awareness and impact, and Creating and leading change
- Section 3 – Maintaining a business focus.

A more detailed guide of what is covered in each section is outlined at the beginning of each section.

Behavioural Framework for Business Partners

Delivering to the business

Holistic overview

- Understands systems thinking and uses this to consider impact of interventions
- Understands the bigger organisational context and future vision and strategy of the company
- Demonstrates a good understanding of the business environment
- Encourages discussions which help identify things stopping the organisation from moving forward
- Strategic thinker – takes a helicopter view on business needs.

Plays many roles successfully

- Is able to flex their skill and experience to suit a wide variety of business needs
- Able to provide both expert advice, and support and guidance appropriately
- Identifies and uses appropriate specialists where boundaries of role end.

Long-term perspective

- Avoids getting bogged down in the operational side of HR work
- Delegates appropriately to others
- Keeps up to date with trends inside and outside the sector which may have business implications
- Helps to shape the direction of the business in line with strategic priorities.

Working alongside managers in the business

Collaboration and empowerment

- Develops good internal networks across their defined area of the business
- Builds and maintains effective relationships with people outside their functional area
- Engages relevant key stakeholders and sponsors
- Actively involves others in the decision-making process
- Ensures that clients are confident and competent to carry on after any intervention.

People-oriented
- Builds strong relationships with clients quickly
- Able to build and maintain rapport with a wide range of people
- Demonstrates empathy and understanding in challenging times
- Builds trust by getting to know clients and their needs well
- Identifies and works with the strengths of others in the team
- Shares knowledge and information with others.

Towards 'win'
- Ensures that contracts are in place for specific areas of work which meet the needs of the client and the business
- Monitors contracts at both the content and the process levels
- Clarifies the boundaries of both their role and the work to be carried out
- Avoids creating unrealistic expectations by their clients
- Acts with political sensitivity towards 'win' situations for individuals and the business.

Self-awareness and impact
Focused on learning
- Questions basic assumptions about self and others in order to heighten learning
- Continually seeks self-improvement
- Demonstrates a good awareness of strengths and areas for development
- Uses learning as a basis for future development
- Seeks opportunities to move out of comfort zone
- Shares learning about the organisation and business issues with others
- Chooses self-development opportunities which are appropriate to needs.

Self-expression
- Actively promotes the business of the organisation through deeds and words
- Demonstrates credibility by understanding the business and the range of issues facing managers
- Resilient – able to cope with the day-to-day pressures
- Able to maintain an appropriate work–life balance
- Presents information in a confident and clear way which meets the needs of the audience.

Dynamism
- Is regarded as someone who 'walks the talk'
- Acts as a role model for others in the organisation
- Engages others by showing a real interest in them as individuals
- Approachable and visible
- Brings visible energy and drive to the role.

Creating and leading change
Proactive and preventive
- Proactively seeks opportunities within the business to support strategy
- Anticipates likely obstacles to implementing business change
- Applies knowledge and understanding of change theory to implement changes successfully
- Strikes an appropriate balance between achieving the business goals and managing emotional reactions to change
- Able to use influence to engage others in the change process.

Innovation and entrepreneurship
- Finds creative ways to work with managers, drawing on a range of methodologies to support business needs
- Able to work independently and make strategic decisions aimed at business improvement
- Looks for and identifies solutions beyond the obvious.

Pathfinding
- Able to cope with ambiguity and complexity
- Role models working on the edge of their own comfort zones
- Identifies new possibilities to take the business forward and create competitive advantage.

Maintaining a business focus
Prioritising
- Places the right priority on business needs in the light of longer-term goals
- Recognises the need to withdraw from a piece of work and moves on without impacting relationships
- Demonstrates an understanding of the difference between urgent and important

- Utilises business data to help shape the direction of the business
- Able to challenge appropriately and say no when necessary.

Utilising feedback
- Actively seeks and reviews feedback as the basis for insight and learning
- Demonstrates learning from feedback by applying new ways of working
- Looks for ways to improve the service of the Business Partner provision
- Seeks to enhance relationships and actions by thorough questioning during reviews.

Demonstrating effectiveness
- Sets appropriate measures at the start of any project
- Ensures buy-in from the business to the evaluation process
- Utilises evaluation data to demonstrate the added value of interventions and the impact on business strategy.

We have included a checklist and a list of references at the end of each chapter as a resource for continuing professional development.

The book aims to be a practical guide which draws on theory rather than an academic piece which may draw on practice. Whether or not we have struck the right balance here is for the reader to decide. We also acknowledge that we have drawn on the work of many others to bring you this book, including our own colleagues and participants on programmes.

We live in a time when there is so much knowledge available to us that it is hard to know where the boundaries are. This in a way parallels the challenges for the Business Partner whose role is becoming increasingly complex. We wish you luck in the challenges, but more importantly we wish you well in your role in delivering a meaningful service to your organisation and its people.

References

Armstrong, M. (1992) 'How to be an Internal Consultant', *Human Resources*, Winter 1992/1993, pp. 26–29.

Block, P. (1981) *Flawless Consulting: A Guide to Getting Your Expertise Used*, Pfeiffer & Company, San Francisco.

Block, P. (2001) *Flawless Consulting*, 2nd Edition, Jossey-Bass/Pfeiffer, San Francisco.

Cockman, P., Evans, B. and Reynolds, P. (1992) *Client-centred Consulting: A Practical Guide for Internal Advisers and Trainers*, McGraw-Hill, London.

Duncan, J. R. and Nixon, M. (1999) 'From Watchdog to Consultant', *Strategic Finance*, Vol. 80, No. 10, pp. 42–46.

Green, M. E. (2002) 'Human Resource Consulting: Why Doesn't Your Staff Get It?', *Public Personnel Management*, Vol. 31, No. 1, pp. 111–20. IPMA International Personnel Management Association.

Harung, H. S. and Reiber, P. C. (1995) 'Core Values Behind 115 Years of Development: A Case Study of GC Reiber & Co., Bergen, Norway', *The TQM Magazine*, Vol. 7, No. 6, pp. 17–24. MCB University Press, ISSN 0945–478X.

Holbeche, L. (1999) *Aligning Human Resources and Business Strategy*, Butterworth-Heinemann, Oxford.

Kenton, B. and Moody, D. (2003) *The Role of the Internal Consultant*, Roffey Park Institute, Horsham.

Laabs, J. J. (1997) 'Stay a Step Ahead with 5 Key Skills', *Workforce*, October, Vol. 76, No. 10, pp. 56–58.

Lawler, E. E. and Mohrman, S. A. (2003) 'HR as a Strategic Partner: What Does it Take to Make it Happen?', *Human Resource Planning*, Vol. 26, No. 3, pp. 15–30.

Lippit, G. and Lippit, R. (1986) *The Consulting Process in Action*, 2nd Edition, Jossey-Bass/Pfeiffer, San Francisco.

McCartney, C. and Holbeche, L. (2003) *The Management Agenda*, Roffey Park Institute, Horsham.

Ulrich, D. (1997) *Human Resource Champions*, Harvard University Press, Boston.

Part 1

Shaping the Business Partnership

The transition from Operational HR to Strategic Business Partnership is a difficult one. Whether you are already working as a Business Partner and are reviewing your effectiveness, or whether your HR function is considering a move to a Partnership model, this part is likely to be of use to you. This part is aimed at helping you think through how to position the Partnership, both from an organisational perspective and as an individual working as a Partner. The chapters focus on how to position and market the Partnership, how to structure and staff the function to suit your organisation and how to target your approach towards your clients.

Chapter 2 examines how Business Partnerships can position themselves to suit both the business strategy and culture. Partnerships need to begin from a starting point of assessing what they are seeking to achieve and influence before they can build their brand image and develop an appropriate marketing plan. The chapter covers how to gain an understanding of the current perceptions of the function and then work to gain clarity on the gap between those perceptions and the desired position of the function. A staged process is presented to help understand the existing client needs and the service provided and advice is given on how to promote the success of the Business Partnership Function by building on value-added case histories.

Chapter 3 examines the various options for structuring a Business Partnership Function depending on the service it chooses to deliver. It examines some of the more practical issues such as what background and qualifications do Business Partners need? How should the Business

Partnership be funded? And what information systems are needed? In addition, the chapter focuses on what organisations are doing to develop and enhance the skills of their Business Partners.

Finally in Chapter 4, we cover how you position yourself as a Business Partner from an individual perspective. The chapter includes topics such as getting established with clients, creating early impressions and how to review the relationships you already have. The notion of different Business Partner roles is explored in more depth and the advantages and disadvantages of working as experts, process consultants or just a pair of hands are discussed. The chapter also presents the CONSULT framework as a way of focusing on the relevant issues when first working with a client.

Some of the key behaviours concerned with delivery to the business (outlined in Chapter 1) will be demonstrated by Business Partners in setting up and positioning themselves in the organisation. Having a holistic overview and long-term perspective are both critical to success in this area, and specific behaviours include 'seeking opportunities within the business to support strategy' and 'having an understanding of the bigger organisational context and future vision of the company'.

2

Positioning the Partnership

Many surveys of HR professionals in recent years have highlighted the priority for HR to become a Business Partner. Yet despite many HR functions seeking to position themselves as Strategic Business Partners working in Partnership with the line, there appear to be few organisations that have made a successful transition to this mode of operation.

It is unlikely that any Business Partnership can succeed unless the HR function has spent time analysing what it is seeking to achieve and how it can add value to the business. While this may seem obvious, it can be easy to re-brand HR without giving sufficient thought to the reasons for doing so. There is also a further step required, which is to promote the aims and benefits of the role within the business. This is a step which, in our experience, is often neglected in organisations and can lead to a lack of understanding and even, at times, resistance from internal clients towards the new Business Partners.

For some organisations, there will be no specific launch of the Business Partnership Function. The new roles might come into existence as part of a wider change programme and may evolve through a restructuring exercise, with some Partners continuing to support old transactional roles during a transition period. For other organisations, launching the new Partnership role and communicating the changes may be the first consultancy project the new service undertakes.

Whether it is a big bang approach or a subtle transition, consideration will need to be given to what the new function is aiming to achieve and how the Business Partnership can promote the work it undertakes and the value it brings to the organisation. To do this, there is a need to understand the perceptions of the people within the organisation, the image and direction the function wants to project and the opportunities there are for developing credibility.

What are You Seeking to Achieve?

Positioning a Business Partnership Function is not a straightforward process. There is undoubted value in having 'inside' agents who understand what is going on, who have strong, established relationships and who are skilled in their interventions. But there are also disadvantages in operating internally and potential consequences to launching a big bang approach to a function if the organisation is not ready for it.

As a first step, it is important to clarify your aims and understand what value you are trying to add by introducing Business Partners. Questions you might ask yourself are:

- Is it just a title change or are there pressing business needs that you hope the Partners will address?
- Why would a consultancy approach be better than other approaches in this situation? (e.g. using external consultants or continuing with the existing service).
- What was missing from previous approaches?
- If the Partnership already exists, what are the current perceptions and what needs does it currently meet?

New Business Partnerships need to be very clear about the business case for moving into this arena. If the Business Partners are not able to articulate the value they can bring or the priorities for the Partners are unclear, then the Partnership is unlikely to be successful.

From the Business Partners we spoke to, the following were cited as business drivers for a move towards Business Partnership:

- Strategic alignment
  - to improve the alignment of people management practice with business goals
  - to help managers understand their people in the context of the organisation.

- Service
  - to provide an accessible point of contact for clients
  - to improve overall service levels.
- Financial
  - to provide improved services at no extra cost
  - to control burgeoning costs on externals.

Most Business Partners felt they were able to offer as good a service as people working externally (sometimes better) and felt frustrated that their clients did not always see them in this light. A possible reason for this might be that the Business Partners do not always spend the time marketing themselves in the same way as external providers. External consultants usually present themselves as a packaged product, with a clear process for achieving results for the organisation. Often with Internal Consultants, the work begins before the potential value is 'sold' to the client.

As a Business Partner you need to be continually viewing your services from the client's perspective and assessing whether you are offering what the client wants. For a Business Partner this may be in the form of:

- *Adding measurable value to the business*: This might be in terms of enhanced customer satisfaction, reduced costs, efficiencies, profits, etc. Tangible improvements in these areas will get clients interested, so presenting your services in this way can be a strong marketing lever.
- *Having a real understanding of the business and the business priorities*: It is important to a client that you show an understanding of their problems and issues. If they need to spend time and effort getting you up to speed on how their area of the business operates, this is likely to reduce their willingness to share their more complex business needs.
- *Focusing on the business critical activities or hot spots*: If you are able to bring some energy and commitment to solving business critical issues, it is likely that a client will be interested in your ideas.
- *Having a strong process for addressing problems*: Knowledge of tools and techniques that can be used to gather data or diagnose a problem is likely to impress a client and reassure them that you know what you are doing. You need to be careful, however, not to use off-the-shelf tools which do not fit the circumstances you are facing and instead develop your own processes that target the issues.

The Business Partnership needs to have a clear focus on what it is offering to the business and the value that brings. You need to be asking yourself, 'Would I want to buy the service I am offering if I was the client?' and 'What am I bringing to the client that they don't already have?'

What are the Cultural Considerations?

Whether your title is that of Business Partner, Internal Consultant, Change Agent or HR Consultant, in our view your understanding of the culture of the organisation and ability to take a big picture approach to working alongside your internal clients will be key to your success. Business Partners might usefully want to develop an understanding of organisational culture and systems thinking skills and processes that are essential in helping to determine the priorities for the Business Partnership.

Before looking in more detail at how the culture might influence the purpose of the Business Partnership, it may be worth reminding ourselves of what culture and systems thinking are about.

The culture of the organisation is often described as 'the way things are done around here'. It is the set of beliefs that govern behaviour in any system – whether that be a family, group or organisation.

In Schein's model of the lily pond (Schein, 1985) the following levels are drawn on to help us understand a broader concept of organisational culture:

- *Level 1*: Visible manifestations of the culture. This is the flower of the lily which shows on the surface
- *Level 2*: Values – these are the stems which support the flower and can be seen through the surface of the water
- *Level 3*: Basic underlying assumptions. The hidden root system which supports and nourishes the plant.

The visible manifestations of culture are the overt signs it is possible to see and hear, including the physical appearance of work spaces and how people are dressed. It also includes the language people use, how written information appears and is produced and what displays of culture there are 'on show' to the public or the outside world. For example, in the

Toyota plant in Cincinnati the work processes are clearly displayed for both employees and visitors to see. Everything is in its right place. The chinos are comfortable but smart clothing and give an impression about how people work with each other and the cars. The values also show through in the 'Toyota way', which means an employee on the assembly line has the right to stop production if they have concerns over how things are progressing. There is a visible pull cord, which is described to visitors during the factory tour. The values in the organisation need to be demonstrated in action as well as words if they are truly to support the overt culture.

The basic underlying assumptions, third level, are more tricky to define, being the roots which are firmly embedded. In strong organisational cultures, the underlying assumptions will, when extroverted, support the values and behaviours. In fragmented cultures the underlying assumptions may be out of kilter with the espoused values of the organisation. For example, if your organisation has an espoused value of 'the customer is always right' and the underlying assumption is 'we get rid of the customer as quickly as possible', something needs attention!

The role of the Business Partner will be to understand how the organisational system works as a whole and where attention needs to be paid to ensure healthy growth for the future.

The following are some pointers for checking on the culture of your own organisation:

- What are the overt signs that tell you what the organisation is like? – for example, environment, layout of rooms, positioning of individuals within the rooms, decorations, what is displayed on the walls, etc.
- How do people treat each other? – are conversations spontaneous and open or are people cautious about what they say and to whom? If someone new comes into the organisation how are they treated?
- What formal and informal processes are in place? – for example: are meetings used as a way of communicating? And if so, how formal or informal are they? What gets discussed? What would never appear on the agenda?
- What groups or cliques exist in the organisation? Is there a real, or an equivalent of, 'golf club?'
- How do decisions get made? And by whom?

- What is valued in the organisation? – getting the work done even if it means staying late? or having a healthy work–life balance?
- Think of a metaphor to describe your organisation and explore this further – for example: if it is like a runaway train, who is driving it? And who are the passengers? What will stop it? Where is it going?

By asking these questions of others in the organisation through your informal networks you can build up a good picture of what the culture of the organisation might be. The culture tends to be determined by the informal rather than the formal processes so do not be fooled by the policies and value statements that are readily available, rather look below the surface at the stems and roots.

Systems Theory and Thinking

In the section above, we have touched on the idea of systems thinking.

> *A system is an entity that maintains its existence and functions as a whole through the interaction of its parts.*
>
> (O'Connor and McDermott, 1997)

A basic, if not in-depth, understanding of systems theory and thinking is, in our view, essential for those working as consultants within organisations, to understand how the interconnecting parts of the business work together and function as a whole. The functioning of the separate parts is important as well as the interconnection of these parts. An easily available, although complex, system to understand is that of the human body.

The body is a healthy system only if the individual parts are functioning properly and work together effectively. For example, someone may have a healthy heart, but if their kidneys do not function well their total health is therefore hampered by the dysfunctioning of one part of the body. Though the heart may be healthy now, because the functioning of the kidneys is vital to overall health the heart will eventually be affected too along with other organs. Anyone with diabetes will know how fluctuating blood sugar levels can affect more than one area of the body.

If we go to our GP with constant headaches, a number of things might happen: We may be asked a series of questions to try to find out what the root cause of the headaches is; we might be given a prescription to stop the headaches; both might happen. The underlying cause of the headaches could be a huge range of things from dehydration to deterioration of eyesight to a dysfunctioning liver, or a combination of all three.

> *Systems have emergent properties that are not found in their parts. You cannot predict the properties of a complete system by taking it to pieces and analysing its parts.*
>
> (O'Connor and McDermott, 1997)

The health and well-being of an organisation is an example of something which is not easily defined. We may know when it is absent – people often talk about low morale in a department or organisation. It may be a combination of many other factors such as changing work structures, high turnover, decreased profits, hostile bids, etc. When the whole system is functioning well and we can see it in action, we will have a better idea of what is going on. Methods such as Appreciative Inquiry (Cooperrider et al., 1999) are aimed at teasing out what works well in a system so that this can be taken forward into the future. By breaking down the component parts and analysing them, we only have a better understanding of the particular part, which in itself is useful, but it will not necessarily aid our understanding of the system as a whole.

Carrying out a cultural and systems analysis will help the Business Partnership to gain a greater understanding of the organisation as a whole and highlight priorities for change.

The model adopted for the Partnership will vary depending on the strategic business objectives of the organisation and the culture needed to support those objectives. Freeman (1997) highlights different ways in which Business Partners can align themselves to the business depending on the strategic objectives of the company (Table 2.1).

Each of these role biases will require a different style and set of skills and competencies from the Business Partners. Understanding the contribution the Business Partner is making to the business and the cultural needs stemming from the strategy is essential in ensuring

Table 2.1 Aligning Business Partnership to the strategy

Strategic objectives	Cultural issues	Business Partner focus
Customer focus	Service levels	Group dynamics
	Team-working	Cross-functional working
	Communication	Team-building
		Clarifying roles/ objectives
		Achieving consensus
Quality/Reliability	Security	Technical consistency
	Professional expertise	Technological improvements
	Attention to detail	Effective procedures
		Creating new solutions
		Knowledge management
Speed of growth	Personal achievement	Complex influencing
	Project based	Strong project management
	Recognising contributors	High flexibility
	Initiative	Responding to stakeholders
Flexibility/ Adaptation	Reputation	Network building
	Freedom to operate	Establishing reputation
	Creativity and risk	Partnerships
	Relationship building	Encouraging risk

Adapted from Freeman (1997)

that the role is focused on areas that add value to the organisation. Many of the Business Partners we spoke to were able to articulate what they were doing (e.g. 'we're trying to facilitate two parts of the business to communicate more effectively with one another'), but were less clear as to whether or not this would make a difference to the strategic objectives. Unless the links between strategy and approach are clear, it is unlikely that the Business Partner will be adding value and they will certainly not have the basis on which to evaluate their success (a topic which is explored in more detail in Chapter 10).

Understand Current Perceptions

Our research suggests that where an Internal Consultancy group exists – particularly where its focus is HR – the members are most likely to identify themselves as junior or middle managers (through pay or grading levels). Usually the consultants are former HR or training specialists who have now been asked to operate under a different business model. Although we found examples of organisations externally recruiting for specific consultancy skill sets, there were only a limited number of organisations taking this approach. The visibility of the Internal Consultant is consequently often based on their hierarchical status, together with their historical position and therefore presents huge challenges in influencing decision-makers (often the clients) at more senior levels. Increasing visibility through effective marketing and self-promotion are a key lever in overcoming this hurdle.

If you are already working as part of a Business Partnership Group within the organisation offering a consultancy service, you will need to consider:

- What reputation already exists about your group?
- What value do we currently bring?
- If you were offering a service under another guise, how might that impact on your credibility for the new service?

If your reputation appears to be based on the people staffing the function, then this might suggest that you need to move away from promoting 'heroes' to promoting a strong process that adds value to the business. If individuals as opposed to the process become branded within your group, then building credibility is down to individuals and is likely to be an uphill battle for HR managers moving across from traditional HR roles.

As much time, effort and resource needs to be put into marketing an internal consultancy as would be needed to establish one providing for an external client base. To quote from Schein (1987):

> *Consultants are typically thought of as outsiders. Even so called internal consultants who work full time for a given company are typically thought of as outsiders to the particular department they are working in at any given time. They are thought of as being free to negotiate their areas of responsibility with others who are defined as clients; they work on a contract basis; they have the power that derives from being an independent outsider and being perceived as an expert in certain areas and they have the freedom to leave a difficult situation except where professional responsibility dictates hanging in.*

Reconciling this view of the role of consultants with how you are currently perceived is a critical milestone on the road to establishing a successful internal consultancy. If you are currently seen as providers of administrative services, however good you are, prospective clients may not consider you for consultancy assignments, as operational credibility may not be a transportable commodity.

Airbus is one company where they 'had to fight really hard to not just become do-ers', particularly as the culture gave credibility to people who implemented change and the other elements of consultancy were not seen as proactive and as a consequence did not build the Partner's credibility. Another Partner in *Zurich Financial* told us 'the main challenge is acceptance by our customers who know us already that we provide more than just an additional pair of hands. We need to constantly ensure that we continue to operate as consultants and not get pulled into the everyday operational needs. This can be difficult when starting from scratch in an organisation that has a "just do it!" mentality.'

Assess Your Brand Image

The advantage that Internal Consultants can be said to have is that they know the business from the inside out. Members of the consultancy team will most likely have lived and breathed the products, financing, staffing issues and business strategies and be well tuned into the hopes, fears, likes and dislikes of the movers and shakers within the business. Paradoxically, the disadvantage for the internal consultancy will also be that they know the business from the inside out! The external consultant may appear to offer something new from another world, whereas the internal consultancy may be associated only with the service they formerly provided. The internal consultancy may also seem to be too entwined with the host organisation's culture and therefore lack the independence and objectivity of the outsider.

A useful first step in marketing Partnership Functions is to carry out some diagnostic work to assess the brand image. *Severn Trent Water* which is part of Severn Trent plc made the move to becoming Business Partners in response to managers saying that they wanted a more strategic contribution from HR. To assess their brand image and focus, they invited in an external consultant from the Chartered Institute of Personnel and Development (CIPD) to give them an idea of how they stacked up against other organisations. Work was also carried out internally with Line Managers, which gave them positive feedback about the current service and what people wanted.

An internal consultancy needs to plan intentional activity to ensure that they align with their brand objectives. This includes how they interact with the business culture; if this is based on status and hierarchy, do they mirror this or make a statement of their independence and freedom by operating in a way that reflects their own values and beliefs about consultancy. If the brand objective is to be seen as independent and objective, the brand statement and action might be 'that we use the most appropriate person to do the job based on their expertise and experience'.

Develop Your Marketing Plan

Positioning the Partnership requires a clear understanding of the business needs and how the service you are offering can meet those needs. There needs to be a clear value in the process you are offering as well as the individuals servicing the Partnership. Often Business Partnerships make the mistake of focusing on *individual* value, at the expense of the value of the *process*, which can impact the perceptions of the function as a whole.

Repackaging and re-branding a Business Partnership needs to follow a number of steps:

1. Assess the need
2. Define the service
3. Test the market
4. Deliver the service
5. 'Brand' the resulting case study.

Step 1: Assess the need

There is no point starting a Business Partnership Function without a clear view of the specific business tasks that require help from HR consultants. You need to prove to yourselves that there is a sizeable need for your service. How big is the need? How many business tasks need help? Where are they located in the business? What are the benefits of doing things your way? As a team you need to have the confidence that you are focused on the needs of your internal customers and not just the HR agenda.

Meislin (1997) offers a checklist for Internal Consultants to use in identifying the help they can provide to their clients.

What do your clients need from you?
1. Client's Name/Business Unit?
2. Who is your client's customer?
3. What type of product or service does your client provide?
4. What is your client's long-term mission or strategic direction? How is it marketing this?
5. Over the next one to two years, what will be your client's biggest marketplace challenge?
6. What kind of help will your client need to face this challenge?
7. How can you help your client to reach short- and long-term business goals?
8. How can you give your client more than standard help? What value-added benefits do you offer above and beyond your role?
9. If you are already working with this person, how do they rate you in terms of satisfaction? What kind of feedback have they given to you?
10. What important points do you need to keep in mind for future work with this client?

You need to discover what the key buying criteria are for your clients and what they value, which means really getting inside the mindset of your clients and understanding them from the inside out.

One of the difficulties Business Partners often face at this stage is deciding who the client is. This topic is covered in more detail in Chapter 3. If the Partnership views their client as predominantly 'the organisation', then it should come as no surprise that individual Line Managers seek the services of external consultants in preference to the internal Business Partners. However, if the Partnership has an overriding aim to impact the culture and strategy of the company, then working solely on Line Managers' agendas is unlikely to lead to success either. Consequently, it is important that the Partnership comes to some agreement about whose agenda they are serving. For example, is a high-level HR need to move the organisation to a more collaborative culture more important than helping your local manager create a smooth transition for a new policy?

Conflicting agendas between the strategy of the Partnership as a whole and the needs of operational Line Managers need to be raised and discussed. Successful partnerships will spend time exploring how they can achieve their client's needs whilst also moving them towards a more strategic vision of what the Partnership is seeking to achieve.

Step 2: Define the service
In order to successfully promote the Partnership unit, you need to be clear on the strategy and direction it is taking. It is a mistake to try and reconfigure an existing in-company service provider into one offering consultancy without addressing the following fundamental business planning issues. Particular issues which are likely to need to be discussed and debated are:

Client issues
- Who are our clients?
- How well do we understand their area of the business?
- What is our current brand image with our clients?
- What are their needs?
- Are they working with us because they think they should or because they value us?

Customer issues

■ How are our customers segmented?

■ Are there policies and practices that make it difficult for them to be successful?

■ What are we offering both individually and collectively?

Products

■ How do our current product offerings impact the business?

■ Where can we add most value to the business?

■ What is the level of demand?

■ Have we got a clear idea of where the greatest need is?

Goals

■ What are we aiming to achieve with the Business Partnership unit?

■ What brand image do we need to support these objectives?

■ Who are our competitors and what do they offer?

Having drawn some conclusions to these questions, you can then begin to frame an overall strategy to enable the unit to be successful. It may be that in discussing these questions it becomes apparent that it may be better to focus on certain services and reduce the service in some areas at the expense of some clients.

A Partnership unit may decide, for example, to focus on upper-middle to senior managers as their clients, as they believe they can add most value at this level and have a stronger influence on the organisation. However, the impact of these decisions needs to be carefully managed if the credibility of the function is to be maintained. If, for example, the unit decides it is no longer providing development centres as the service is too costly and time-consuming, the rationale for this needs to be effectively communicated to the business and an alternative supplier sourced if necessary. The alternative is that the team agree amongst themselves and when a development centre is next in demand they lose credibility by not being able to deliver, or offer a means of delivering, a solution. Word can soon spread within a company that a business unit is not able to help meet people's needs.

It is important that the Business Partnership documents the service it will provide. This avoids a Business Partner turning up to their first client meeting with just a big smile and a blank piece of paper. If the Partnership Function has developed a clear process that is proven to add value to the business then both Business Partners and their clients will feel confident that working together on a consulting project will add value and leave best practice behind. *The Body Shop* is an example of a company who spent a lot of time considering how to market themselves internally. They worked as a team to develop a service and then positioned it as led by senior managers.

They came up with the name 'The LADS' which stood for Leadership And Development Section and was catchy enough to get them known within the organisation and signal that a change had taken place. The team saw themselves on a continuum from dependency to independence to interdependency or Partnership. They mapped this out as a way of plotting their relationship with Line Managers and this eventually became the path they took holistically with the organisation as a whole.

They received extensive external and internal Marketing advice and established a Brand and Image – and used the power of metaphor to capture the passion and imagination of their learners. The following is an extract from their write-up of the experience (Inside Outreach Ltd, 2002).

To build a common sense of what we were trying to achieve we created the image of the learner as an independent explorer and traveller, not a passive spectator. Our slogan was 'Learning is for Life . . . not just for courses' and we used this extensively in our materials and marketing literature.

When we were clear about our offering, we mounted a campaign for learning and we used a lot of visual imagery which fitted into the Body Shop culture and visual environment – with quotations like E M Forster's: 'Spoon feeding teaches you nothing but the shape of the spoon' strategically placed over the canteen servery. Plus we had the Board Directors team giving out Passports to Learning at the factory gates at 6.00 a.m. on a cold January morning!!

The care we put into our image alongside delivering the goods really paid off. We had some clear messages about our offer and what we were doing to disseminate information within the organisation and beyond and we were well published in the internal communications and external press. There was a great motivation and enthusiasm

---

> *amongst the team – success bred success. All the work we did had a positive impact and got reinforced. We particularly impacted through the design and delivery of a suite of management development programmes – with the innovative approaches moving the thinking more towards a learning culture.*

Step 3: Test the market

Once you have assessed the need and clearly defined a service to meet that need, then you can test the market and refine your service as appropriate. An initial high-profile project can be a good way to develop a proven case study, which can then be used as a solid foundation for gaining credibility and further work.

The approach you can take to marketing your function will be influenced to a large degree by the culture of the organisation and the readiness of the clients. It is likely that your internal clients will have a wide range of reactions to your role as Business Partner. Figure 2.1 illustrates how clients progress in terms of their perceptions of the role:

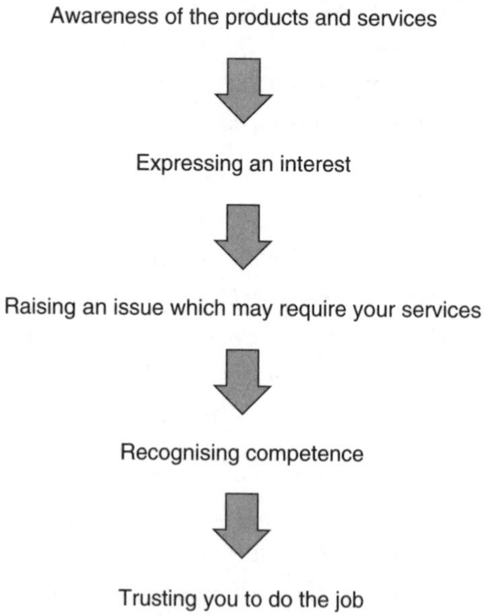

Awareness of the products and services

⬇

Expressing an interest

⬇

Raising an issue which may require your services

⬇

Recognising competence

⬇

Trusting you to do the job

Figure 2.1 Client's perceptions of the Business Partnership role

Your marketing approach will obviously need to be targeted at the appropriate level. Initially, this may mean a focus on raising awareness on the role and what service you can provide. Case studies and presentations targeted towards their critical business issues will be a way forward here. If however, a client is already beginning to question you and raise issues of importance to them, then the approach will need to be quite different and you can start to use consultancy skills to draw out the client and demonstrate your process expertise.

Pfizer are an example of one company who have successfully marketed the transition of the HR role to that of Internal Consultants. They used Ulrich's matrix (1997), which was described in Chapter 1, as a basis for charting their progress. Starting from a strong operational focus where the HR section worked as employee champion and focusing on quality policies and processes to support this, they began by gaining a greater understanding of the business and its goals and drivers and started to build relationships and credibility with key players. This enabled them to move to a more strategic focus where they could challenge thinking and help facilitate discussions on the future of the organisation. Having achieved this, they then moved on to concentrate on the senior leaders in the organisation and focus on culture change. The move was not without resistance and the team drew in external consultants to help take the pressure off the internals and enhance their credibility by using others to reinforce their approach.

Step 4: Deliver the service

The service you deliver will vary hugely depending on your role and remit. We pay more attention to the interventions you might be involved in Chapter 8.

Step 5: 'Brand' the resulting case study

If your market testing is successful then you will have a successful case study to launch your new brand image. Ideally, you will want to choose a case study that is seen as a hot topic or critical to the business. Thereafter, the Partnership needs a constant and relevant message to the business to maintain a successful profile.

Tapping into existing promotional opportunities is essential in this activity and numerous avenues are available which should be used as building blocks for communication.

Written marketing materials
Brochures, report presentations, past case studies and articles in company newsletters are all useful in raising the profile of the Business Partnership. Stories of your success are particularly valuable in developing your credibility with the business.

Workshops/breakfast meetings
These can be used to brief managers on the services on offer and help raise awareness on the role of the Business Partner.

Conferences and seminars
Talking at slots on management conferences about specific projects. Presenting alongside an external speaker can also help raise your profile.

Networking events
It is essential that Business Partners get out into the business and get seen. This means taking advantage of all opportunities to informally network across the organisation. Professional institutes such as the CIPD and IMC also hold events which provide an ideal opportunity to network externally with other Business Partners and gain useful insights into your work.

Web
Intranet sites can be particularly useful as a marketing tool, especially when the department is being set up or where potential clients are not aware of the capabilities on offer. This can sometimes be the case where an organisation works across different locations. The *Immigration Authority* uses the intranet for managers to download HR policies and also to access interactive training, where managers self-select HR issues and receive question and answer support.

Logos and brand names
Logos can be useful to create a brand for the function, but you need to be careful that they symbolise what the function does. There may also be trademarks, such as Investors in People which are important to include. A distinct identity can be useful in informing the organisation about what you stand for or what you offer.

Coca-Cola found that the credibility of their Partnership Function could be influenced by something as simple as the name given to a particular project. As a result of this they ensured they selected unique and unambiguous names and had a clearly identified leader for each piece of work.

Testimonials
Make sure you get positive testimonials for your work. Word-of-mouth referrals are one of the best ways to get new business. Where you are seeking to get a start in a new market, it can be useful to hold a pilot in an area that you know will be successful and use this as a stepping-stone to other areas of the business.

Gifts
Items which symbolise or remind managers and employees about the work you are trying to achieve are a useful way of raising awareness. *Nortel*, for example, gave out a wooden puzzle with a core competency on each piece at the end of a briefing programme, to symbolise that each employee has at least one strength and that each piece is important. The puzzle was cheap to produce and kept the model in the forefront of people's minds (Morris, 1996).

Summary

Positioning the Business Partnership Function requires a clear understanding of the business needs and how the service you are offering can meet those needs. Whilst the move to a Partnership model may be driven by financial, service or strategic imperatives, the value the Partnership brings will depend on whether the priorities it establishes are correct and whether the Business Partners themselves are able to influence change.

Gaining a thorough understanding of the culture and systems of the organisation is essential not only because Business Partners need to understand how they can influence strategic change, but also because the cultural dynamics of the organisation will have an impact on the shape of the role the Business Partner plays. Fast-growing companies focused on flexibility and personal achievement, for example, will require a stronger project management focus and more complex relationship management skills; whereas companies with a more established, quality-driven culture are more likely to value a focus on procedural improvements.

Our experience shows that internal consultancies rarely put as much time and effort into promoting themselves to their clients as external providers, and yet often there is confusion about what the function is seeking to accomplish and the process for achieving it. Partnerships can benefit from taking time to understand the existing perceptions of their function within the business and examining the brand image they are promoting. The gap between this image and the service they are seeking to deliver can then be established.

The starting point for any marketing plan needs to be an analysis of the client's needs. With Business Partners this is often not straightforward, as they frequently have split loyalties between line management needs and the needs of the business as a whole. Balancing those needs and setting clear priorities is the first step in defining what the Partnership is about and what it is aiming to achieve.

A strong brand image can then be built by offering a service which meets the business needs and uses case study examples and promotional opportunities within the business to reinforce simple messages about the Business Partnership Function.

Checklist

Key considerations for positioning the Partnership:

- What are the business drivers for moving to a Partnership model?
- What are the strategic objectives you need to align with?
- How well does the Partnership role support the cultural aims of the business?
- Can you articulate what you can offer your clients?
- What are your client's perceptions of you and your role?
- What brand image are you seeking to achieve?
- What service do you provide?
- How clear is your marketing strategy?
- Where is your client positioned in terms of your role?
- What successes can you market as case studies?
- How effectively do you leverage the promotional opportunities open to you?

References

Cooperrider, D. L., Sorensen, P. F., Whitney, D. and Yaeger, T. F. (1999) *Appreciative Inquiry: Rethinking Human Organization Toward a Positive Theory of Change*, Stipes, Champaign Illinois.

Freeman, C. (1997) 'Training Your HR Pros to Fit Your Culture', *HR Focus*, Vol. 74, No. 5, May, pp. 9–10.

Inside Outreach Ltd (2002) see www.inside-outreach.co.uk.

Meislin, M. (1997) *The Internal Consultant: Drawing on Inside Expertise*, Crisp Publications, Menlo Park.

Morris, D. (1996) 'Using Competency Development Tools as a Strategy for Change in Human Resource Function: A Case Study', *Human Resource Management*, Vol. 35, No. 1, pp. 35–51.

O'Connor, J. and McDermott, I. (1997) '*The Art of Systems Thinking: Essential Skills for Creativity and Problem Solving*', Thorsons, London.

Schein, E. H. (1985) *Organisational Culture and Leadership*, Jossey-Bass, San Francisco.

Schein, E. H. (1987) *Process Consultation*, Vol. II, Addison-Wesley, Cambridge, Mass.

Ulrich, D. (1997) *Human Resource Champions*, Harvard University Press, Boston.

3

Setting Up the Partnership Function

Within any organisation there will be choices to be made about how to structure and staff the Business Partnership. If the business drivers and client needs discussed in the previous chapter are clear, then this may already provide an indication of how best to set up the function. However, structures and staffing issues often emerge from the existing shape of the organisation, rather than being designed to meet a particular need. This chapter is aimed at exploring the implications of different structural models as well as highlighting what is happening in practice within organisations.

The chapter seeks to address questions such as:

- What are the advantages and disadvantages of different structural models?
- Where should the Business Partnership be located?
- How should the department be funded?
- What role do information systems play?
- What background do Business Partners need?
- What development might be needed?
- What reporting structures work best?
- Are external consultants still of value?

What are the Options on How Partnerships Should be Structured?

What service do you deliver?

Lawler and Mohrman (2003) highlight an obvious dilemma that HR functions face when they attempt to become more strategic, in that 'HR is not in a position to abandon completely the basic transactional responsibilities associated with workforce management'. Mercer HR Consulting (Griffiths, 2004) also state that there is a general recognition that more business understanding is needed in HR, but suggest that HR need to prove they can deliver effective and efficient service on the administrative functions before they are able to make the transition to supporting top priority business needs.

Consequently, to be effective a number of different aspects need to change and also be perceived to have changed by the organisation. These include not only the work that is being undertaken by HR, but also the skills of the individuals in the HR function; the way the function is structured and the way it promotes its services and interacts with the key stakeholders of the company.

Lawler and Mohrman (2003) argue that to be successful, companies need to first find a way to provide an effective transactional service. This may be through:

- Outsourcing the day-to-day administrative functions
- More effective use of Information Technology (IT)
- Devolving responsibility to line management for HR processes.

This will then free up time for HR to participate in strategy development, change processes and implementation. However, if the transactional HR tasks are not adequately provided for, then it will be almost impossible for HR to break away from the more reactive nature of these tasks. Their longitudinal study of HR within organisations backed up this argument and found that where HR was a full Business Partner they had a far higher level of activity in areas of planning, organisational design and organisational development.

One of the first tasks in shifting to a Business Partnership model is therefore to establish the effective delivery of transactional HR activities. Increasingly, organisations are rushing into strategic HR partnerships at the expense of operational, day-to-day HR services and as a result are instantly losing credibility (Pfau and Cundiff, 2002). As part of the research for this book one business manager told us that their move towards Business Partnership included re-branding the HR function as 'Providing Excellence', but this was viewed as a joke within the organisation as they appeared unable to do something as simple as issuing an accurate offer letter following a successful interview. Whilst many Partners will want to move away from the transactional HR, it is still essential that the basics are in place before the transition occurs.

Ulrich (1997) also warns against taking a fixed view of the role of HR and focusing on the business value roles of strategic partner and change agent at the expense of the role of administrative expert and employee champion. He argued that even if the administrative role sits inside a service centre or operates as an outsourced function, it still needs to partner with the organisation in some respects. However, if we are talking about Business Partners working as strategic partners, influencing change through process consulting, how should organisations go about structuring their HR function to best effect? The nature of the company will play a key role in finding the answer to this question, but some of the more typical models we uncovered in our research are outlined below.

Model 1: Business Partners as process consultants working alongside the line, with specialist and transactional HR provided centrally or outsourced

This model has the advantage that Business Partners are able to develop strong working relationships with line management and have a good knowledge of the business issues they are facing, as well as the resources at their disposal. The Business Partner adds value by working as a process consultant, coaching and mentoring managers and helping to diagnose business problems and develop solutions. Where specialist advice is needed, such as for employee relations or reward strategies, they are able to call in expertise from the centre.

If the centralised transactional HR function is efficient and effective then this model should work well. However it also relies on Line Managers recognising the value of process consultants and allowing the Business Partner to get involved in strategic issues when they do not have expert advice to give.

Barclays was one company we spoke to which followed this model. They introduced a Business Partnership model for HR in the latter part of 2001 as part of a move away from a decentralised HR set-up. The new model has three components:

1. A centralised HR Service Centre which carries out the transactional HR processes.
2. Centres of excellence which are comprised of groups of specialist advisors working in two main areas, namely:
   (a) Resourcing and learning
   (b) HR specialist practice which covers:
       - equality and diversity
       - talent management
       - pensions.
   These centres of excellence have evolved over the last few years. Their prime role is to develop policy and processes to support the business, but they also have a delivery capability.
3. The Business Partner team who work alongside the business operation.

Of the 72 000 people in Barclays, approximately 1000 are in HR. Of these, roughly 400 are in the Service Centre and there are about 130 Business Partners.

Prudential are another organisation cited in People Management (2004) as following this model. They have Business Partners working as consultants and they draw on expertise from the centre, whilst a service centre deals with the administration. The Business Partners do not have their own budget, but use the advice of HR experts who do. A key part of the role is therefore to be able to influence others without budgetary power.

Shared Service Centres are becoming increasingly attractive to large organisations. The *National Trust* recently moved to a shared service centre model to reduce the amount of time HR spent on routine queries. They have an intranet site containing information on employee benefits and a service centre to answer personal queries on benefits. If these are not answered they are referred to the Regional HR Directors.

However, as the person on the ground, it can be difficult to separate yourself from the day-to-day HR activities. Even if this is achieved, one Business Partner from the *Hyde Group* highlighted to us that once they successfully managed to separate themselves from the transactional HR problems, they found that they were disadvantaged on occasions as they still needed to be in close contact with what was going on. *Zurich Financial* have overcome this to a certain extent by setting up a 'Solutions Consultancy' where the Business Partners contract with transactional and specialist HR teams when they require assistance. This has the advantage of clarifying the role boundaries whilst ensuring communication is kept open when required.

Model 2: Business Partners as process and specialist providers
working alongside the line, with transactional HR reporting in to them
This model suggests that Business Partners work in an expert role as well as that of a process consultant, which is likely to be an easier transition in companies not familiar with the benefits of process consulting. The Business Partner has a higher status in HR and keeps in touch with the day-to-day activities by having the transactional HR roles reporting to them.

The *Immigration Office* have recently moved to this model of Business Partnership. They set up a service which provided more strategic alignment to the business, with expertise in areas such as organisational design, performance management, reward strategy and job evaluation. The response was very enthusiastic and positive and as a result an Interim Manager was brought in to trial the Business Partner approach. This was done in one of the most challenging areas of the organisation – National Asylum Support Services – which had a history of difficult HR challenges.

Despite preparing the Directors for what service might be on offer, the newly appointed Business Partner soon got dragged into HR operational problems. So to counteract this, HR Advisors were appointed to work for the Business Partner and unblock the operational issues. The pilot ran for around six months with the Business Partner working on areas such as change strategy and workforce predictions and the HR Advisors providing back-up on the operational issues. After the pilot period there were plenty of success stories and the Business Partnership role was expanded to other parts of the business.

Within the Immigration Authority, there are now eight operating Directorates each of which has a Business Partner with a Senior Advisor as well as other HR Advisors reporting to them. The Business Partner has line management responsibility for the HR Advisors. The Senior HR Advisor role is to identify HR hot spots in the business and track records of HR and as such, it is more of a junior Business Partner.

One of the possible difficulties with this model, which was highlighted in the Immigration Office case, is that Business Partners may find it difficult to distance themselves from the transactional HR activities, particularly if they are perceived as the next level in command. In addition, playing both expert and process roles may lead to unclear role boundaries and difficulties setting expectations with clients.

Model 3: Business Partners as process consultants working alongside the line, with specialist and transactional HR provided centrally and a local HR Advisor as a focal point for transactional issues

In this model the Business Partner is free to operate strategically as there is a separate port of call locally for transactional HR issues. The two roles can also keep in close contact to familiarise each other with the key issues. Once again, this model relies on an effective central provision of HR services and a clear understanding by line management of the value a Business Partner can bring. It has the benefit, however, of not leaving Line Managers feeling unsupported in terms of operational HR and not creating a hierarchy between Business Partners and Operational HR.

Royal Bank of Scotland is one company, which has a similar approach to this model. They not only have a shared service centre for HR administration, but also have HR consultants (Business Partners); HR technical experts in areas such as reward, resourcing and organisational development; and HR analysts working alongside Line Managers in the business. There is a close link between the two roles with the HR Analysts providing data on topics such as sick absence and turnover to help the consultants with their analysis of problems.

Model 4: Business Partners working alongside the line on specialist and transactional issues using a process consulting approach

This model, where a senior HR professional takes an all-encompassing role and works closely with line management is likely to be the way forward for smaller organisations which do not have a requirement for large HR service centres. The work differs little from that of more traditional HR Managers and what changes there are have come about in the way of working with managers, whereby the Business Partners are more facilitative and aim to develop self-sufficiency amongst the line.

Canon Europe have taken a similar approach to this. They do not have a separate HR service centre and instead each country has an HR Director/Manager; Senior Business Partner; Business Partner; HR Specialist and administrators.

The model has the advantage that all the HR functions are closely in touch with the business. However, the role definitions may be much less clear as a result. In several of the larger organisations we talked to, it was hard to see a clear transition towards Business Partner despite the change in job title. In those cases, the HR professionals were struggling to make time to be proactive with the business due to their heavy operational workload. This suggested to us that whilst this model may work in smaller organisations, or in companies with small business units, it is unlikely to generate change or be perceived as adding strategic value in a larger company unless the individuals themselves are very assertive about their role.

Choosing an Appropriate Structure

These models indicate that ideally Business Partners should be seeking:

- A strong working relationship with the line
- Good knowledge of local business issues
- Intelligent clients who understand the value of process consulting
- The ability to access strategic issues
- Clear role boundaries with transactional HR
- The ability to pull in expertise when required.

Not all of these factors are likely to be in place however. So choosing an appropriate structure will depend on the existing perceptions of HR and the experience of Line Managers in working in a process consulting style with HR. Table 3.1 gives a rough indication of the characteristics that need to be in place for each of the models to work.

Table 3.1 Structuring the Business Partnership

Model	Factors which need to be in place	Benefits
Model 1		
Business Partners as process consultants, with specialist and transactional HR provided centrally or outsourced	■ Effective central or outsourced provision of transactional HR ■ Line Managers understand and value process consulting ■ Business Partners able to access strategic issues	■ Ability to build strong working relationships ■ Gains an in-depth understanding of the business issues ■ Ideally positioned to influence change without distractions
Model 2		
Business Partners as process and specialist providers, with transactional HR reporting in to them	■ Effective provision of transactional HR is close to the line ■ Line Managers value specialist input along with process consulting ■ Business Partners establish clear role boundaries with transactional HR	■ In touch with the day-to-day HR issues ■ Ability to tailor the specialist advice directly to the client ■ Ability to build strong working relationships ■ Gains an in-depth understanding of the business issues
Model 3		
Business Partners as process consultants, with specialist and transactional HR provided centrally and a local HR Advisor as a focal point for transactional issues	■ Line Managers understand and value process consulting ■ Effective central provision of specialist services ■ Business Partners able to access strategic issues ■ Status issues are clarified	■ Line Managers feel supported on transactional issues ■ Ability to build strong working relationships ■ Gains an in-depth understanding of the business issues

(Continued)

Table 3.1   Structuring the Business Partnership—Cont'd

Model	Factors which need to be in place	Benefits
Model 4		
Business Partners working alongside the line on specialist and transactional issues using a process consulting approach	■ Line Managers need a one-stop service ■ Transactional issues are interlinked with specialist advice and strategic intent	■ Suited to a smaller organisation ■ Involvement in all areas gives a greater understanding of the whole

Location

The location of the Business Partnership will obviously depend on the structure of the company. *Coca-Cola*, for example, decided it was important to get as close as possible to the business and it operates in a decentralised way out of more than 23 sites in the UK each of which has a local HR resource. The *Immigration Authority*, however, are geographically spread across the UK, but are divided up functionally rather than regionally as the differing functions have very different needs. As a consequence, they may have two Business Partners quite close together regionally but who offer services to two very different directorates.

When deciding on the optimum location, it is important to consider where everyone in the marketplace is located, including:

■ Internal clients
■ Internal customers
■ External customers
■ Key stakeholders
■ Suppliers.

To be effective, Business Partnerships need to find an appropriate balance between the centralised functions of the business and the strategic business units. The best location will depend on what your customers need from you, how close you need to be to the key stakeholders to have an influence and where you can best add value to the business.

Cargill are an example of one company who have changed the location of their Business Partners to enable them to focus more on their HR strategy. Cargill employs around 110 000 people globally and the HR function is currently structured along the lines of Model 1 (see Table 3.1). It is split into three broad areas:

1. **Shared service provision** – a global unit with a regional person based in Europe
2. **HR in Europe** – HR Business Partners embedded in the business who work on the strategic business agenda
3. **Specialists** – who provide expertise in core areas.

They have been operating the above structure for four years, but previously they were working by country. Whilst some countries still have a country HR provision, Cargill found that this model did not drive into the key HR issues and people ended up providing the day-to-day shared service functions. The transition has not been easy and there are still some areas of the business where people are hanging onto their old jobs, refusing to give up what they see as power. As a consequence, turnover has been high in the last three years and they have moved people so that they can make the changes they want to see. However, they now have a structure where expertise is used well. The Business Partners work in true partnership with the specialists and they are able to sell a more holistic service to the business.

Funding

The way in which the Partnership Function is funded will have a big impact on the evaluation process. As a support function there are obvious choices between being centrally funded as an overhead or charging for the services across the organisation. Service level agreements, call-off contracts, project fees and pricing agreements are all possible ways in which the charging of the Business Partnership can take place. Some companies set their costs by estimating the number of consultancy days required and setting annual contracts.

Charging for services may seem a natural progression for HR activities where they are linked to the bottom line. It helps to show how the business can respond to competition from outside the organisation, as well as clearly demonstrating the value added by the function.

PowerGen, for example, have a zero profit–target HR centre which charges at cost for its services across the organisation. The charges are set by examining the size of the business unit and the amount of change taking place. All of their customers are free to use other suppliers, and they have found themselves bidding against external providers for some services and occasionally losing the business (Hall, 1995).

Some partnership groups also undertake some fee-earning work outside the organisation with varying levels of success. *IBM* set up an external profit-making HR company called 'Workforce Solutions,' which they found made them more innovative as a service provider. They eventually sold off the business despite its success as they found they were spending too much time costing solutions and marketing a cost-effective service rather than focusing on the service that would add most value to the business. Other organisations, such as *Xerox*, *Walt Disney Corporation* and *Pacific Bell*, have made more of a success of selling HR expertise externally. They found they were increasingly being asked to provide benchmarking information and this led to them selling their expertise. The value they have gained is not only professional recognition, but also an ability to learn from their customers (Laabs, 1995). Interestingly, for Xerox, the move meant that the HR function was re-aligned under sales and marketing as a product of the company.

In our view, if the function is not charged out then the work is often undervalued and perceived as a cost which can be cut. However, excessive charging can also lead to competition with external consultants, which can waste a lot of time and focus the work of the Business Partnership away from their core role. One large banking group changed their charging system when it became evident that their work was shifting towards areas of the business that had the budget to pay, away from parts of the business where they could really add value. As a consequence of these difficulties, Neubaum recommends that a cost should be charged to cover the overheads, but a profit element should not be included.

Information systems

Aside from helping to speed up the transactional HR activities, advanced Information systems have also been found to be a key lever in becoming a strategic partner. Good IT systems enable HR to gather strategic data and analyse information in different ways. As a result Business Partners can explore issues and contribute to finding solutions in a more informed and business-focused way. Lawler and Mohrman's study found a strong correlation between a completely integrated HR Information System and a Strategic Partnership role. This was echoed in the study by Pfau and Cundiff (2002), which also found that an e-HR strategy focused on improving accuracy, upgrading services and transactional interrogation was of more value to the bottom line than one focused on enhancing communications or promoting culture change.

Staffing Issues

Background and qualifications

Mercer HR Consulting's survey of HR professionals (Griffiths, 2004) indicated that most organisations were more likely to invest in the HR staff that they currently employed and then develop business understanding and cross-functional experience amongst those staff. In our research, however, this seemed to be more the case for companies beginning the transition to Business Partner and as the function got more established, there appeared to be a trend towards broadening the background of Partners beyond HR and bringing in more consultancy expertise.

One reason for this may be that many HR professionals lack assertiveness and self-belief (People Management, 2004) and there is consequently a large gap between existing HR staff and the skills needed to be Business Partners. In consultancy, individuals need to be able to challenge the presenting problem and influence change and they need to have the confidence to do this without having the status to help them.

In some organisations we surveyed, such as *Severn Trent Water* and *Barclays*, the background of their Business partners was mixed, with some coming from within the existing HR structure and some coming in from outside. A Business Partner we spoke to at Barclays had noticed an increasing trend to move away from the more traditional CIPD background which about 50 per cent of the staff hold. The ability to diagnose, influence and coach was seen as equally, if not more, important than extensive HR knowledge. Severn Trent Water have recently appointed an HR Advisor with an engineering background who is 'transitioning' into the HR role, which signals to the business that Business Partners are not all pure HR people. They want to give the message out that they welcome people in from different backgrounds.

However, in other organisations, such as the Immigration Authority, CIPD qualifications are an important criteria. For them, transforming the role of the HR Advisors was challenging and it was important that people were seen as credible with the relevant qualifications. Ideally they are aiming for all Business Partners to have CIPD qualifications and accreditation from the IMC following a course on consultancy practices.

The Business Partner must feel confident in their role and the power vested in them to be able to give difficult feedback to senior managers when appropriate. A lack of confidence or lack of positional authority can lead to ineffective interventions, with the fear of credibility leading the consultant to make more expert judgements. There are particular issues for those moving from specialist functions such as training, personnel or operational management to consultancy. Business Partners do not always have positional power, particularly if their primary role is not that of Internal Consultant and they are performing this role as an additional function. The HR specialist who moves into the role must learn to deal with the ambiguity and frustration that will inevitably come from a lack of positional power.

In considering who is appropriate for the role, organisations should consider which people in their team would convince them to shift their thinking? If they would not convince you, how will they convince others? As there is quite a different skill set required (which is discussed in more detail in Part 2), it is clear that not everyone in the 'old' HR teams are likely to be deemed suitable for the new business consultancy role. As a consequence, it is important to consider if the skills can be built internally or whether you will need to recruit people with an existing skill set, as in the case of the Immigration Authority. There may also be people in other areas of the organisation who have key skills/expertise that could be trained in the consultancy role and would benefit from being developed in this way.

Experts or generalists?

All Business Partners need to be expert in the skills needed to consult effectively with clients. The level of subject expertise needed will depend on the role the Business Partner is playing (see Chapter 4) and there are inherent dangers in setting yourself up as an expert in a particular field. However, it is likely that for most large partnership projects a mix of generalist skills and expert input will be required. Whether this expertise comes from the Business Partner or from elsewhere in the HR function is less critical and will depend on the structural model for the Partnership.

Reporting lines

Business Partners reporting lines vary. Some organisations favour a dotted line to HR with a solid reporting line to the business unit, whilst in others it is the reverse – with a solid line to HR and dotted to the business manager. Whichever set-up is used, it is important to be clear on who is driving the priorities for the Business Partner and clearly establish where the priorities should lie.

Reporting lines for the Head of the Partnership Function can also be critical. Ideally they would report directly to the Chief Executive or Chief Operating Officer. This will not only give the function more visibility and a higher level of sponsorship, but also provide the function with more political pressure if required. Reporting through another HR Director or through the Business Unit Directors will create certain expectations about what will be delivered and will be a less influential position.

Use of project teams

In order to address complex business issues, it is likely that for key projects there will be a need to bring together a combination of people with a mix of knowledge and skills. When working in teams, there is an added value in involving line management as well as the HR Partners, as this will provide a level of involvement and buy-in to assist in any implementation actions. However, teams bring with them inherent difficulties in terms of how business projects are managed. When working in teams, the Business Partners need to be clear on:

- Who does what
- How you interact with the client
- How you communicate with each other
- How you monitor progress and update each other

Use of external suppliers

Effective partnerships have been found to make better use of external resources and will contract in specific capabilities or expertise as a way of strengthening their own position. Freelance consultants, OD Associates and Academics can all bring specialist skills and experience to a project that may not be present within the organisations. Effective Business Partners often hold a budget to enable them to bring in such people and they are not afraid of this damaging their own credibility.

If external resources are drawn in to work on a project, even when Business Partners are not the budget holders, it is critical that they are involved in the selection process and setting the scope of the external's work. Aside from this preventing misunderstandings or duplication of effort, it will also ensure that the Business Partner is more committed to making the contract a success.

Fujitsu are one company who draw on external partners to help them in their work. They undertook a recent project on talent management and used external suppliers to help them to profile the role. This resulted in a recruitment campaign plus an Academy for identifying internal talent, looking for 'internal stand-alone leaders', which was all part of a strategy to get the right people in the right roles.

Experience of the Head

Studies have found that the Senior Executive in charge of an HR Business Partnership Function are most effective if they have an HR background themselves, as well as a good knowledge of the business. People who transfer into the role from the business often have difficulty understanding how HR can contribute effectively to strategy development and implementation (Lawler and Mohrman, 2003).

Training and development

Many companies, such as *Shell*, have chosen to run tailored training in order to enhance their internal consultancy skills and develop more effective service providers. The staff in Shell People Services predominantly had HR generalist backgrounds, having worked in several operating environments both within and outside Shell. However, some had not had much prior experience of internal consultancy. To address this they developed a consultancy skills programme, covering the role of a consultant and the techniques and frameworks of effective consultancy.

It also covered a range of issues such as influencing others, interpersonal awareness and personal presence. The modular course, designed and run by Roffey Park, allowed the participants to put theory into practice in the workplace and share experiences as a group.

Most companies also focus on increasing business awareness and understanding and some, such as *Royal Bank of Scotland*, provide financial training to help HR become more focused on the bottom line issues. University partnerships are also being used to support development. At the *Prudential*, Business Partners are trained in strategic thinking at their own University and the *Civil Service* has linked with Kingston University to provide a Master's degree in HR Strategy and Change to help their transition to Business Partnership.

Companies with more established Business Partnership roles, such as Royal Bank of Scotland and *Shell*, have also carried out considerable work into defining roles and competency requirements. *HBOS* have their own HR development centre and Shell have competencies and job profiles to help HR staff identify paths for career development. In the next part, we will focus on the key behaviours required for Business Partners.

Providing development opportunities
It may be appropriate to rotate people from the business through the function, to provide not only a development opportunity for the individual, but also a new business insight into the project. Rotation of key managers from the business can have an added value in that it enhances the organisation's knowledge about what the Partnership Function's role is and how it can have a positive impact on the business. However, there is a danger in this approach, as people new to the role are unlikely to be skilled in the consultant behaviours required to be most effective and as such may lack influence and credibility.

Longer-term postings, typically one to three years, are a good compromise and have the benefit of bringing new skills and knowledge from the business into the Partnership Function, as well as broadening the consulting capabilities of the individuals. This is not easy to achieve however, as Line Managers are often unwilling to take long-term secondments without the security of a post on their return to the business. It is imperative that any placements are not used as a way of 'finding a hole' for managers who are surplus to requirements, and that the positions are viewed as a developmental step for high-potential staff.

Depending on the size of the organisation, there may also be value in rotating HR staff through different aspects of HR and Operational Management, which is much easier to achieve. This will provide them with a more rounded picture of the different aspects of the business and a greater understanding of how different HR activities can add value.

In some more international companies, such as *Cargill*, there is a need to ensure that the Business Partners gain a broad cultural understanding of the different companies and gain more exposure to the acquisitions across Europe. They have developed the skills of their Business Partners in a number of ways:

- Several people have moved to different countries
- HR have been given real responsibilities in the Business Units
- Using the London Business School
- Visiting sites, for example in Germany, to get close to the customers
- Young people are brought in and trained on new assignments
- Appointing a coach or mentor outside their own area, for example across shared services and HR Business Units.

Summary

A number of different models exist for structuring Business Partnerships. Some structures encourage stronger client relationships due to the close proximity and focus on the process of consulting, whilst others bring in more specialist advice and a closer relationship with transactional HR activities. The size of the organisation, the effectiveness of the existing transactional HR provision, as well as the core business drivers and client needs will all be factors in deciding on an appropriate structure.

Business Partnerships need to be located where they can add most value to the business. This is likely to depend on where the key stakeholders are positioned and what your clients need from you. Reporting to either the HR or the Business Unit Director also has significant implications in terms of the expectations and priorities of the role.

Whilst some of the Partnership groups we came across charge for their services and even carry out work outside the organisation, it is more common for groups to work as an overhead in a traditional HR charging structure. This has implications for Business Partners in that it sends a message to the organisation about the value the function brings and may mean that Business Partners need to invest more time raising their profile and building credibility. Ironically, bringing in external suppliers with new expertise can often help Business Partners build their own credibility.

Information systems have been found to have a large impact on the ability of Business Partners to operate strategically. Companies can use IT to speed up transactional activities and thus free up time for more strategic work, as well as enabling HR to gather and analyse strategic information in new ways.

Business Partners do not always start with positional power in organisations and, as a consequence, the ability of the Business Partner to influence strategic change is often more likely to stem from individual confidence and interpersonal behaviours than a particular background or qualification. In our research we noted an increased trend to move away from more traditional HR qualifications, to individuals skilled in a consultancy approach. Much of the training and development being undertaken is also aimed at enhancing consulting skills, as well as developing increased business understanding.

Checklist

Key considerations for structuring and staffing the Partnership:

- How effectively are transactional HR activities currently managed?
- What types of specialist expertise are required?
- How effectively do HR Information Systems support and capture data on the business?
- How strong are the relationships with the line?
- Where are the key clients and stakeholders located?
- Is process consulting understood and valued in the business?
- What level of experience does the existing HR team have?
- What particular expertise is required to assist the business?
- Are the existing teams able to access strategic issues?
- How will project teams be managed?
- How will costs be charged?
- How strong are the external networks to key resources?
- How will the communication links with transactional HR be managed?

References

Griffiths, J. (2004) 'Partnership Drives Worldwide Change' [Mercer HR Consulting], *People Management*, Vol. 10, No. 7, p. 12.

Hall, L. (1995) 'Pay Your Way', *Personnel Today*, 18th July.

Laabs, J. J. (1995) 'HR for Profit: Selling Expertise', *Personnel Journal*, Vol. 74, No. 5, pp. 84–88.

Lawler, E. and Mohrman, S. (2003) 'HR as a Strategic Partner: What Does It Take to Make It Happen?', *Human Resource Planning*, Vol. 26, No. 3, pp. 15–30.

Neumann, J. E., Kellner, K. and Dawson-Shepherd, A. (1997) *Developing Organisational Consultancy*, Routledge, London.

People Management (2004) *One Step Beyond*, June, pp. 27–31.

Pfau, B. N. and Cundiff, B. B. (2002) '7 Steps Before Strategy', *Workforce*, Vol. 81, No. 12, November, pp. 40–44.

Ulrich, D. (1997) *Human Resource Champions*, Harvard University Press, Boston.

4

Positioning Yourself with the Client

Challenge for Existing HR Personnel

In the preceding two chapters we have focused on positioning the Partnership Function and giving consideration to issues around how the function is structured, resourced and marketed. These could be considered to be at the hard edge of Business Partnering. Equally important, in our view, are the process issues around the relationships you need to build with your internal clients and the client system as a whole. The way each individual Business Partner positions themselves within the organisation is critical to the success of the function as a whole.

One of the key challenges facing those who go into the Business Partner role from an existing HR position is that of influencing cultural change. Being part of the organisation brings both advantages and disadvantages: whilst having a strong understanding of prevailing cultural norms, internal agents may also be 'blind' to them. With often only their own personal power and influence as tools, those working internally may also fail to account for the extent to which they contribute to sustaining the culture which they hope to change. High self-awareness appears to be a key requirement for anyone working inside the organisation in this way.

Credibility comes in many forms. It can come with a good track record – so Business Partners who have been in HR in a previous role, may or may not have a good track record. Those recruited from outside the organisation may be at an advantage here in that there is no previous history. However, they will have to work harder at understanding the politics and culture of the organisation.

Getting in!

The term 'gaining entry' is commonly used when referring to the early stages of a consultant–client relationship. It is equally valid if your title is Business Partner. The title, as we have illustrated elsewhere, does make a difference in that 'Business Partner' infers a level of strategic intervention, so this is preferable to some other HR-related titles. The term 'Internal Consultant' is also still commonly used. The title is one way in which perceptions of people using the service can be influenced. If you have the title 'Strategic Business Partner' with the back-up of a seat at senior board meetings, you are already off to a good start for building relationships and credibility.

We refer to the term 'gaining entry' here to examine the access that an individual has within the organisation, as well as the level to which they establish and maintain effective relationships with their internal clients. Gaining entry also means having a level of visibility within the organisation; being clear about what services you are offering and how you will work with your clients – specifically, the benefits of your service to them and the organisation.

Some key questions to gauge your existing level of influence:

- Do people in the organisation know who you are?
- What image comes to mind when they think about you or your group?
- What services will you offer to your clients?
- How do they know what is available?
- What is the nature of the contract that you will have with them? – that is, do you work to service-level agreements? Or what other standards can they expect?

Many of the people we have spoken to in organisations (apart from those with the title 'Business Partner') are still unfamiliar with the term and do not know what it means and how exactly it relates to the business.

At the 'gaining entry' and relationship-building stage (as well as at other stages in working with clients), it will be important for the internal Business Partner to act like an external. By this we mean approaching your clients as if you were selling your services to them. In some cases this will be exactly what happens under service-level agreements. In others, the cost and time issues are less clear so it will be important to behave 'as if' you were being paid directly by your client for the work that you do.

Early impressions

The first impression you create with anyone, client or potential client (as they are all in that category), is of paramount importance. In the world of external consultancy, it is often the make or break time. If the client responds well to you on a personal level, you are more likely to 'win' the work. Internally, you may be contracted to carry out work with a client, but if there is little rapport between you both, you may find relationships becoming strained or non-existent. Rapport can be gained in a number of ways such as:

- Demonstrating knowledge and understanding of the client on a personal level
- Demonstrating knowledge and understanding of the client's area of the organisation and business issues affecting their work
- Mirroring aspects of body language
- Matching verbal language, style and tone of the client
- Matching other aspects of personality (e.g. level of directness, generalisations, attention to specifics and detail or concepts and ideas).

Some people feel uncomfortable about matching and mirroring as a way of gaining rapport. However, it is important to remember that you are not mimicking! – and the intention is key. If you have respect for your clients, which comes from a belief that you will have a better relationship with them if they feel you are on their wavelength, you are more likely to do this in a way that feels congruent. Just notice how much you need to match and mirror so that the dialogue feels comfortable for you both.

Client's Readiness and Capability

The ability of the Business Partner to gain entry also depends on the client's readiness and capability for change (Beckhard and Harris, 1987). Often, a move into a consultancy role and away from operational support will mean a significant change for the internal client. For example, if managers have been used to personal contact with someone from HR to deal with personnel issues which have now been transferred to a call centre, the shift in role will represent a significant change. Rather than a one-to-one meeting with someone to talk through problems/organisational issues, the manager may now have two or three people to contact about different aspects. In addition, the manager might need to deal with personnel issues themselves, with little skill or capability to do this.

An example in one organisation we spoke to included the discomfort some managers had around dealing with 'HR issues'. Investigation by the HR team showed that there was a capability issue around the managers being able to deal confidently with poor performers. Unofficial HR teams had been set up locally to support managers but the advice they provided, which included options for how to proceed, did not deal with the underlying issue of managers' lack of skill in dealing with poor performance consistently.

Beckhard and Harris's model for assessing the client's readiness and capability for change is useful here:

- Assess the attitudes of key stakeholders towards the change – willingness, motives and aims = readiness
- Analyse the power sources, influence and authority issues, and skills and information required = capability.

Some of the steps we recommended in the previous chapters will help you to determine the levels of both readiness and capability. If the Business Partnership Function is to be successful, some internal consultancy on your internal consultancy is necessary!

The readiness and capability equation can also be applied to those moving into the consultancy role as primary stakeholders in the change. It will be important to assess current levels of capability and skill amongst this group and find out what development needs they have at an early stage – preferably skilling them up or recruiting suitable people in before services are offered.

As part of assessing the client's readiness and capability, the Internal Consultant can consider what else needs to happen towards successful change. Force-field analysis is a familiar change model, which can be applied to consider how to move from a present position to a desired future state. An example of how this might look for the transition to Business Partnership is shown in Figure 4.1. In this example some of the

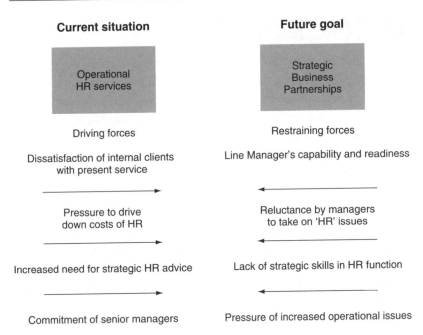

Current situation

Operational
HR services

Future goal

Strategic
Business
Partnerships

Driving forces

Dissatisfaction of internal clients
with present service

Pressure to drive
down costs of HR

Increased need for strategic HR advice

Commitment of senior managers

Restraining forces

Line Manager's capability and readiness

Reluctance by managers
to take on 'HR' issues

Lack of strategic skills in HR function

Pressure of increased operational issues

Figure 4.1 Transition to Business Partnerships

areas that appear as driving forces could be resisting forces, for example Senior Management commitment may not be present in your organisation. It is usually easier to change restraining forces, since when you increase the driving forces, people may feel pushed and become even more resistant. Having said that, some of the driving forces (particularly financial) can be so compelling that they help to force the changes needed.

Force-field analysis can help at the early stages of establishing a Business Partnership in many ways:

- It can help to uncover potential obstacles and reveal what is really blocking the proposed changes
- It can help anticipate special factors to take into account in preparing for implementation
- It helps to identify sources of support that you may not have previously considered.

After analysing the driving and resisting forces, it is important to think about actions for both minimising the resisting forces and increasing the driving forces.

65

Business Partner Roles Re-visited

We touched on roles in Chapter 1. Another perspective on the roles you might find yourself taking is drawn from the world of consulting.

Many of you will be familiar with the doctor–patient metaphor as a way of describing the consultant role. Where consultants have previously been regarded as an 'expert' through their specialist roles, they may find themselves inadvertently providing expert solutions to clients who still perceive them in this way.

Expert or Doctor–patient role

In the expert role, the client places the responsibility for identifying the root cause of the problem and subsequent solutions in the hands of the consultant or Business Partner. The client is likely to take a passive role and in this way the relationship can also take on parent–child like qualities in transactional analysis terms (Berne, 1993), with the client/child playing up from time to time. However, this role can have some advantages for both the consultant and the client. It can be a good way to 'gain entry' for the Business Partner. If you have been known for supplying a particular expert service and are seen to be credible, you have an added advantage of existing good relationships with clients who will have valued you for the service provided. For the client it can provide a huge sense of relief to know that someone is prepared to 'take on' your problem and sort it out for you. However, at either a conscious or subconscious level, clients may also think that if something does not work out, they have a ready-made scapegoat to protect their credibility and reputation. Once in this role, attempting to get the client to accept ownership and responsibility for the problem/issue can be tricky and attempts by the consultant to release themselves from this expert role can cause anxiety for both consultant and client.

Many of the people working inside the organisation in a 'consultancy' capacity readily identify with the role of expert or doctor–patient.

Pair of hands or purchase–supply role

This is the role next most commonly identified by those people we have worked with inside the organisation. In the research carried out by Roffey Park in 2003 (Kenton and Moody, 2003), we asked what the key challenges were facing those working internally. They were:

- Being presented with the solution which someone thinks is right to implement rather than being allowed to research the issue/problem and complete a full consultancy process
- Actually being able to operate as consultants as opposed to project leaders
- Having to work hard to push their way in and work alongside managers so that they can create project plans.

Working as a 'pair of hands' usually means the power and responsibility lies with the client who invites you in to provide some solutions for which you have perceived expertise. Again, there are advantages and disadvantages, although many we spoke to would see this as an undesirable role. A clear disadvantage would be in creating an expectation within the client that you will always work with them in this way and not being included in the early and important discussions and decisions about organisational development. It is a transactional rather than a transformational role and those truly working at a strategic level in the organisation are less likely to be used in this way.

Process consultation/collaborative role

This is the role many Business Partners will aspire towards mainly because in this role, responsibility and ownership rest equally with you and your client. Each party sees that they have expertise and experience that will be of value in the relationship and they contract to work together in joint problem-solving and diagnosis. This clearly has some advantages, particularly in helping organisations to manage change. To be seen as an equal contributor in identifying organisational issues and likely ways forward, rather than expert or implementer, means that the client is truly viewing you as a valued partner. If, however, you are to work in this way, certain competencies are key – including good self-awareness; skill in working with process issues; being comfortable with ambiguity and an ability to challenge clients constructively if you feel you are being enticed into other roles!

In order to work collaboratively, the client as well as the Business Partner must be capable and ready to work in this way. This, in turn, demands a set of values and behaviours for working which may be quite different from previous ways of working with internal service providers. If, for example, the client does not perceive a need for improvement, and/or the client does not have the appropriate problem-solving skills to engage in joint diagnosis, then working in this way will prove very difficult. In addition, some of the structural models for Business Partnerships outlined in the previous chapter will prove unworkable.

The extent to which cultural values of collaboration, open dialogue and self-awareness prevail has a key impact on positioning the client's relationship within the intervention. So an important need exists for Business Partners to check out the client's readiness to 'devote time, energy and the committed involvement of the appropriate people to a problem solving process' (Lippit and Lippit, 1986).

There are several factors which may impact on the success of the Business Partner to work collaboratively with the client.

'Internal Customer' values: On the face of it, it might seem that a strong 'internal customer' value would align well with Business Partner activities. However, in practice this manifests itself through the tensions inherent in meeting the perceived need of the customer, framed as it often is by the customer's need for a speedy solution.

Relating this high customer-focused value to the consultant roles determined by Schein (1987) shows the challenges this can bring for an Internal Consultant (Table 4.1).

In some cases a clear distinction between the concept of 'customer' and 'client' has not been established when developing a Business Partner Function: rather one approach has overlain the other, causing confusion in both the Business Partner's expectation of their role, and the client's expectation of the working relationships. One example highlighted this: in a large manufacturing company, an internal consultancy group had been established to provide HR interventions at divisional levels. As the group developed an awareness of their role, they began to understand where providing solutions (to what were often complex people issues) did not help the client in the long term. In fact, these actions were helping to create a higher level of dependency – particularly once the client had built a strong relationship with the consultant and 'knew where to go' with an issue. Whilst individual consultants recognised the need to move towards a process consultancy role, the message from their manager, a Director, was that the Internal Customer model of working should prevail. This leads to frustration and raises questions about the strategic relevance of creating the consultancy group.

Table 4.1   Consultant role

Consultant role	High internal service expectation
Expert	■ Delivers solution quickly without high client involvement ■ Customer needs met early ■ Lacks systemic approach to diagnosing ■ The presenting problem may not be real issue
Pair of hands	■ Reasonably aligned with high customer-focused values ■ Focused on meeting customer needs ■ Power lies with customer, though the customer's perception of the issue may be 'wrong' ■ Not possible to challenge customer's assumptions as customer is 'right'
Process	■ Working collaboratively may be construed as 'passing the buck' ■ Customer expectations for solutions may not be met within the desired time frame

A Framework for Working Collaboratively

At the beginning of any relationship, it will be important to identify some key areas to help provide a focus before taking more substantial steps.

The following framework can help Business Partners work together with their clients to establish what the issues are and what actions might need to be taken. In this way it might provide a basis for a contracting discussion with the client. The beliefs that underpin this framework are closely aligned to those of process or collaborative consulting. The aim is to help the client think through the nature of the problem or issue they are facing and to find out if the client is truly committed to finding a way forward by asking questions and listening carefully to the response. The framework can be used as a mental checklist over the period of a project, as well as a checklist for a one-off conversation.

CONSULT stands for:

■ Context
■ Overview

- Needs of the client
- Symptoms
- Underlying issues
- Long-term likely effects
- Tasks and timescales.

Context

Here, the Business Partner finds out about the context of what is needed. Information is gathered about the area of the organisation in which the client works, so that the consultant has a clearer picture for going forward. Normally, you will already have a good or developing understanding of the business; however, it will be important not to make assumptions and rather let the client confirm the context from their own perspective. This is also a good opportunity to find out how this area of the business links to others. As well as a fact-finding discussion for your benefit, it can help to raise the client's awareness of the interface between their work and the work of other sections.

Questions for consideration:

- What is the main purpose of the team/unit?
- How many people are there?
- Where are people situated geographically?
- What are the differing sections/departments and how do they relate to one another?
- Who are the clients/customers? (as appropriate)
- What methods of communication are in place?
- What other processes and systems are used? (asking about areas of specific relevance)

Overview

Get an overview of the situation as described by the client. This will be the first presentation of the 'problem' as defined by the client and so it will be useful to pay attention to how the client describes what is happening. How open are they about what they understand to be happening? – What is unsaid? – What do you notice about their emotional level as they describe the situation to you? This overview will provide the bigger context before getting more detail.

Questions for consideration:

- What are the issues for discussion?
- What is happening at the moment?
- What has led up to this situation?
- Who is involved?
- How did this come about?

Needs

The needs of the client should be identified. They may say they want you to come up with the solution – in some way to 'fix' the problem. Again, notice how they define their needs. What is said and what is implied will give you a good clue on their expectations of you and how they might want to work with you. They are also likely to have emotional needs of, for example, reassurance. If you pick this up at an early stage it might be appropriate to give some reassurance in the form of empathy – 'it sounds like this has been a difficult time for you' or 'you've clearly put a lot of energy into this so far'. This might sound obvious, but active listening and empathy are sometimes forgotten in either anxiety or enthusiasm to find out exactly what the problem is and how you are going to solve it! At this stage you need to go slow to go fast. In other words, do not jump to conclusions about how this issue might be resolved.

Questions for consideration:

- What does the client need from you?
- What has already been thought about/tried out?
- What has prompted the client to take action now?
- What would make this situation better for the client and others?
- How might some of the explicit and implicit needs of the client be met by you?

Symptoms

What are the overt symptoms the clients have noticed, which have brought them to asking you for help? Examples might include customer complaints, arguments between staff, system failure, increased error rates/costs, reduction in quality, hostile competition, etc. Symptoms are distinct from signs in that they tend to be more overt and identifiable results of problems or issues.

Questions for consideration:

- What has the client noticed specifically, which is happening in relation to this issue?
- What examples are there of particular problems/issues?
- Specifically, what is causing this to be a cause for concern?
- Where is the problem? And where it is not?
- How has it impacted on other areas of the business? – What have they noticed?

Underlying issues

You will need to have an understanding of the issues that underlie the situation as outlined by the client. As these tend to be less obvious than the overt symptoms, the client may not know or fully understand these at this stage. Underlying issues may emerge only once work has begun; however, it will be important to have a sense of the underlying issues as things progress and for both the client and the Business Partner to be fully appreciative of all the causes. For example, an issue of team morale may emerge to be more about the pay and reward system than conflicting relationships between team members. Having a diagnostic framework in mind, which encompasses soft and hard areas, will help at this stage.

Questions for consideration:

- What else is contributing to this problem or issue?
- What is the problem with the problem?
- What happened just before this became an issue?

Long-term likely effect

How much of an issue is this for the client and the organisation? Paying some attention to this area will help you to establish the level of commitment the client has to engaging in the change process. If you sense at this stage that there is little engagement or little impact if the issue continues, you will have some clues about the priority of this in the client's perception.

Questions for consideration:

- What is the likely impact if this issue continues?
- In what way do you see this as impacting on the business?
- If this continues, what is likely to happen?
- If we do nothing, what is the likely impact?
- How does this affect your bottom line?
- How is business likely to improve if this is tackled effectively?

Tasks and timescales

What are the steps you agree to take next? This area is about being clear on the boundaries for the next stages of working and might include an initial contract between the consultant and the client on further information-gathering/diagnostic activity.

Questions for consideration:

- What needs to happen next?
- What are the milestones to be agreed?
- What activities will be important?
- Who needs to do what and by when?
- Who else needs to be involved?
- What constraints do we need to be aware of?

As with any framework, this needs to be applied flexibly. It will be rare for the client to follow the order this framework sets out and you will need to match where the client is and skillfully steer back to any areas which you feel are missing. Do not feel you have to cover all these areas in one conversation. It may be more helpful to have these areas in mind as a backdrop to the longer-term relationship with your client.

Reviewing the Relationship from Different Perspectives

There are four main themes to have in mind for reviewing your discussions with the client:

1. What is the issue?
2. What do you know, think and feel about the issue?

3. How does the client see things from their perspective?
4. What would be an organisational take on the issue?

You will invariably be starting from your own perspective. If you have received a letter, e-mail or phone call – you may already have some assumptions about the issue, more so when working inside the organisation. This can be a useful source of information to draw on for a better understanding of what is going on. This is commonly known as the first-person perspective.

From your discussions with the client – how do they see things? – using CONSULT what have you found out about their hopes and fears and outcomes they want from working with you? Why is this issue important to them? Looking at it from this angle is known as the second-person perspective.

Imagine now the organisation takes on a persona – what would they be saying about the issue, bearing in mind what else is happening in the organisation. Here you are aiming to look at the issue from a more detached perspective rather than getting back into your own views and assumptions. Where does this view come from? And what is it based on? – how much in touch are you with the organisation as distinct from perhaps one or two influential people on the Executive Board? This is from a third-person perspective.

Finally, as an objective consultant to yourself, from a fourth-person perspective, what advice would you recommend to yourself for working with this client?

Clients, sponsors and stakeholders

In the early stages of the relationship it will be important for Business Partners to establish the key players for the piece of work presented. An understanding of stakeholder management will be helpful here.

The client will normally be the person who has presented an issue to you. However, the client system will include everyone in the organisation potentially. So the question 'who is the client?' is an interesting and important one. If the person who presents the issue to you is not at the most senior levels of the organisation, it is always worth considering their manager as another potential client who might need to be engaged in conversations about the issue at some stage.

Sponsors

A sponsor will usually be someone at a senior level of the organisation who agrees or volunteers to 'champion' a piece of work. In some organisations, the project planning approach requires each piece to have a sponsor. In our experience the role of the sponsor is not always clear. Again, the following questions might help to clarify the need for a sponsor and the role they would play.

- Does the issue impact on the organisation at every level?
- Does it impact significantly on the future of the organisation? – either the way work is carried out or the products offered?
- Will it require shifts in attitude or behaviours at the most senior levels?
- Will it require support from senior managers, even if it does not affect them directly?
- What are the risks of this project if there is no visible sponsor to support the work?

If a sponsor is named – either because it fits in with your company's approach to project planning or because you feel this would be useful – we would recommend a contracting discussion with the individual at an early stage. This ensures you are clear about how the sponsor will actively support the work as it unfolds. Often sponsors are so in name only, with little clarity about how they should perform the role. Sponsors could be encouraged to be active in their role in the following ways:

- Making a presentation to launch an initiative
- Holding open forums for question and answer sessions
- Attending planning meetings to give active support
- Adding their views on written communications such as updates on project progress
- Kicking off training and development programmes or attending to end-of-programme presentations.

Stakeholders

A simple and useful way to determine the key stakeholders is to consider:

- Who knows?
- Who cares?
- Who can?

These questions (Revans, 1980) make reference to stakeholder groups in terms of those who have information about the organisation, its history and current culture, and/or about the presenting issue.

They include people who have been in the organisation for some time and could be at any level of authority – the priests and storytellers referred to by Deal and Kennedy (1982). These are the people 'who know'. Those stakeholders 'who care' would include anyone with a vested interest in contributing to the work or with an interest in the outcomes. These people may or may not have power and influence – but it is worth asking yourself, 'What is the risk of leaving them out of the research/consultation process?' The final category are the people 'who can' – which includes those with financial or positional authority who have the potential to either help or hinder the progress of the work. A simple framework can be applied to analyse stakeholders and determine where you need to spend your energy as a Business Partner (Figure 4.2).

Commitment and support will be evident in what people say about the project or issue you are trying to influence and also in their deeds. Are they prepared to commit time and energy to supporting this work?

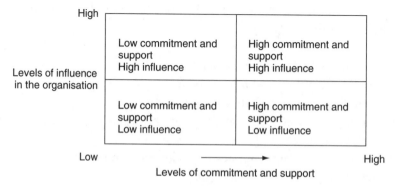

Figure 4.2 Analysing your stakeholders

Levels of influence in the organisation can be determined by some of the following:

- Is this person responsible for making strategic decisions in the organisation which affect the way the business is run?
- Does this person get listened to by people in the above category?
- Do they have a senior role in the organisation?
- Are they interpersonally persuasive and credible?
- Are they seen to be a good role model of management in the company?
- Do they have responsibility for a substantial budget linked to your project?
- Can they give this project the 'go ahead' or put a block on action that might need to be taken?
- Do they 'have the ear' of the Chief Executive or others on the Senior Management Board?

Based on levels of commitment, support and influence, you can decide on the priorities for stakeholder involvement. For example, where you have senior managers who are highly committed and in an influential position, how can they be used to support the changes that are needed? For example, a decision to go into partnership with another company clearly needs to have senior management support.

The influential supporters can be used to communicate positive messages about the benefits of the partnership to the organisation. Clearly, energy needs to be placed in the low commitment/high influence arena, as the drawbacks of either not getting support here or active opposition could be risky. If this is the case, it would be worth finding out the cause of the lack of commitment. These senior managers may have some very valid reasons for not supporting the changes more actively. How can you work to minimise the resistance or use it constructively?

You will probably not want to spend time and energy on those who have little commitment and little influence. However, those with commitment to the issue and low influence might usefully be used as a lever for others. Also, you will want to keep them engaged and involved, so in managing the work, you might want to consider if they can actively be engaged in running events or carrying out research.

Relationship mapping

Another useful way to analyse the relationships you have with your internal clients is to spend some time in mapping the relationships. This can be done either for a specific project or for your internal relationships more generally. The example that follows is based on an NHS client seeking engagement of senior managers in the diversity action planning process (Figure 4.3).

Stage one: Map out the key people or groups who have a vested interest in the issue.

Stage two: Using the commitment and influence matrix, identify who is in which category (as far as you are able).

Stage three: Highlight in some way the degree to which you have an effective relationship with them – this can be done by showing solid or dotted lines to that person or group of people. ('Effective' means are you getting what you need from them and vice versa.

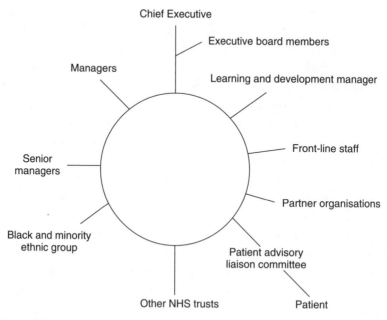

Figure 4.3 Stakeholder mapping

If you do not know what is needed, this could prompt a conversation to find out.)

Stage four: Finally, make an action plan to spend time on the relationships that are critical to the success of the project.

Another way to use the relationship map is to help you think about the relationships you have with your wider client system.

Networking is another form of gaining entry, which is key to the success of the Business Partner role. Networks need to be built at an early stage and paid attention to throughout for effective practice. We return to the subject of networking in Chapter 6.

Promoting Yourself

Often marketing yourself is not considered to be an active part of the role of Business Partner. Your clients may be chosen for you and there may be little scope to influence the projects you work on. Whether it is perceived as part of your role or not, your ability to influence change in the organisation will be driven to a large extent by your ability to get involved in the right projects, with the right people. One Business Partner we spoke to commented that there was a vast difference between the effectiveness of the function and the way Business Partners carried out their role across the organisation. Where the perception of the individual and their ability to access value-added projects is in question, they are less likely to be effective.

Business Partners who have moved internally into the role from a more traditional HR structure will find the need to market themselves and promote their own capability – a radical change to their previous role. However, if your organisation and the key managers within it are largely unaware of the change in role and what it means for them, it is highly unlikely you will be able to discuss problems and work in a collaborative way with clients. Your clients will need to understand what you can offer and have the confidence in your abilities to deliver.

Depending on the structure, there may be more or less of a need to market the services provided, but in some cases the internal partners will be competing on a level footing with external providers and will therefore need a more aggressive approach to marketing themselves.

When the Business Partner has been recruited from a more traditional structure where there was a captive market for their services, this is even more of a significant change to their role and skill set.

One of the first steps in promoting yourself is to try to get a better understanding of your role and the contribution you bring. Key questions to reflect on are:

- What are your key skills?
- What is unique about you?
- How do you operate to best effect?
- What values and beliefs do you have that drive your work?
- What are your personal objectives as a Business Partner?

Lift test!

Often you will be given a short opportunity to 'sell' what you do to people you meet in the organisation. Thinking through an eloquent and informative response to the question 'so what's your role?' will stand you in good stead. This is sometimes referred to as the 'lift test'.

The lift test is a good way of gauging if you are clear enough about what you do – to be able to describe it to someone in the time it would take the lift to go from one floor to another. Write it down, practice it and test it out to make sure you can 'sell' what you offer within the business – clearly and succinctly. Does it say something about you and the way you like to work, as well as the outputs you deliver?

Summary

The early stages of any relationship are key to its success. Whether we are talking about a lifetime partnership or important business relationships, how you position yourself with the client and within the client system is a fundamentally important part of your overall role. The key things to consider here are: convincing yourself that you have something to offer; being clear about what that is; and having the confidence to project that to others.

Gaining entry is not just about having the confidence to network and let people know who you are and what you do, but also about having sufficient interest in all parts of the overall system (i.e. the organisation), to want to know how the interlinking parts connect and how individuals within the organisation work. It also means having a genuine interest in others and developing a curiosity about them as individuals as well as part of the overall system.

There is a difference between a client and a customer and if organisations have a culture and set of values in place which places the customer at the forefront of thinking, your internal clients might need to come to terms with accepting a balance between meeting their needs and the wider needs of the organisation. This means clear communication about the role of the Business Partner and the relationship between you and your internal clients.

Before jumping to conclusions about what needs to happen in any given situation presented by your clients, it will be important to get the background information and find out 'what is going on around here?' both in the way the client describes the situation to you and from your own take on what is happening. Utilising a framework such as the CONSULT model, described in this chapter, can help to ensure that the Business Partner digs deeper into the issues being presented.

This part has paid attention to the early stages of shaping the Business Partnership, which are crucial to its success. Paying attention to developing key relationships as well as the structural and positioning issues will help to make sure your internal clients are on board with the changes. Building good relationships with your clients is perhaps one of the most important skills of the Internal Consultant. Once trust and rapport are established, an effective working relationship can emerge.

Checklist

- Are you providing expert advice only on those areas where you have sufficient expertise?
- Are your clients building their own knowledge and understanding through the process of working with you?
- Are any of your clients becoming overly dependent?
- Do the values of the organisation support your desired ways of working?
- Are you establishing the underlying cause for issues presented to you by clients?

- Are you identifying the key stakeholders – Who knows? Who cares? And who can?
- Have you contracted with sponsors as well as your clients about their role?
- How engaged are your clients at the outset of discussions?
- Are you involved in early discussions on business strategy with other senior managers?
- Have you identified all the key stakeholders in your current projects?
- Are you engaging stakeholders and using them to help influence others in the organisation?
- Have you built networks and are you maintaining them effectively?
- Are you networking with senior managers and those with influence in the organisation?
- Are you spending time finding out about people and who they are as individuals as well as what their business issues are?
- What else do you need to do to raise your profile and credibility within the organisation?

References

Beckhard, R. and Harris, R. (1987) *Organisational Transformations: Managing Complex Change*, Addison-Wesley, Reading, Mass.

Berne, E. (1993) *What Do You Say after You Say Hello?*, Transworld Publishers Ltd, London.

Deal, T. and Kennedy, A. (1982) *Corporate Cultures: The Rites and Rituals of Corporate Life*, Penguin Books, London.

Kenton, B. and Moody, D. (2003) *The Role of the Internal Consultant*, Roffey Park Institute, Horsham.

Lippit, G. and Lippit, R. (1986) *The Consulting Process in Action*, 2nd Edition, Jossey-Bass/Pfeiffer, San Francisco.

Revans, R. W. (1980) *Action Learning: New Techniques for Management*, Blond and Briggs, London.

Schein, E. H. (1987) *Process Consultation*, Vol. II, Addison-Wesley, Cambridge, Mass.

Part 2

Developing the Key Skills

The main focus of this part is on developing the key skills needed to work effectively at a more strategic level within the organisation. If we consider the behaviours in the framework shown in Chapter 1, plus any role-specific skills linked to particular specialisms (such as compensation and benefits), the list is somewhat daunting. Here we will focus on skills which we consider paramount to the role; in particular consultancy skills, reflective practice, political and relationship skills and the skills in leading and influencing change.

Chapter 5 focuses on consultancy skills by looking briefly at the consultancy cycle as a backdrop to working inside organisations and providing a client-centred approach. The rest of this chapter concentrates on the art and science of contracting and highlights considerations around whom to contract with, issues to cover in the contracting process and how to avoid some of the pitfalls.

Chapter 6 examines the importance of self-awareness and self-reflection in the client–consultant relationship. This really highlights some of the complexity around the nature of working inside the organisation and encourages Business Partners to take time both during their interventions with clients and afterwards to make sense of what is going on. The chapter also highlights some of the key considerations when dealing with the internal politics in the organisation and the importance of networking.

Chapter 7 continues a theme we refer to throughout the book about the importance of maintaining good client relations – in particular developing rapport, establishing and maintaining trust, building credibility and dealing with pressures effectively along the way.

The final chapter in this part (Chapter 8) looks at creating and leading change and the role of the Business Partner in acting as a catalyst towards organisational transformation. We take examples from Business Partners of value-added interventions to show the scope and range of work, which could truly epitomise what the role can encompass. In this chapter we also look at the challenges that present themselves in trying to influence change from a position inside the organisation.

Some of the skills outlined in our model in Chapter 1 which are included in this part are that the Business Partner: 'Ensures that contracts are in place for specific areas of work which meet the needs of the client and the business'; 'Proactively seeks opportunities within the business to support strategy'; 'Anticipates likely obstacles to implementing business change'; 'Finds creative ways to work with managers, drawing on a range of methodologies to support business needs'; is 'Able to cope with ambiguity and complexity'; 'Identifies new possibilities to take the business forward and create competitive advantage', plus many of the behaviours under self-awareness and impact.

5

Key Consultancy Skills

The Business Partner role has many similarities to that of an Internal Consultant and as a consequence many of the consultancy skills are included in the behavioural framework we have developed. In order to get a better understanding of consultancy skills, this chapter outlines one of the commonly used frameworks for consultancy and focuses on some of the key skills applicable to Business Partners, in particular the need to contract effectively with clients.

What is Consultancy?

Before exploring consultancy skills, it is worth revisiting some of the definitions outlined in the Introduction. There are many differing definitions of consultancy and depending on the primary purpose of your role, different definitions will have a lesser or greater 'fit'. However, all consultancies will in some way have the purpose of providing help to a client and for the purposes of this chapter, a simple definition provides us with a focus:

> *A 2-way interaction – a process of seeking, giving and receiving help.*
> (Lippit and Lippit, 1986)

or

> *A person in a position to have some influence over an individual, group or organisation, but who has no direct power to make changes.*
> (Block, 2000)

As we explore the skills in more depth, you will see that the role can be complex and so you may like to develop your own definition and understanding of consultancy in the context in which you work. Having this understanding of what consultancy means can help us to be clear with our clients about the service we aim to provide.

The Consultancy Cycle

Consultancy skills are often described with reference to the life cycle of a project. Figure 5.1 shows how the consultancy cycle typically appears (Cockman, Evans and Reynolds, 1992).

Each of the stages shown in Figure 5.1 highlights skills needed by the practitioner.

Phase 1 – Gaining entry

This phase involves being able to build good rapport with your clients and establish credibility and visibility within the wider client system. It includes a whole range of sub-skills: being sensitive to client needs; effective communication and influencing skills; and the ability to attend to both the content and the process of communication.

Whilst Internal Consultants may have their projects given to them rather than having to sell themselves to gain a piece of work, the initial

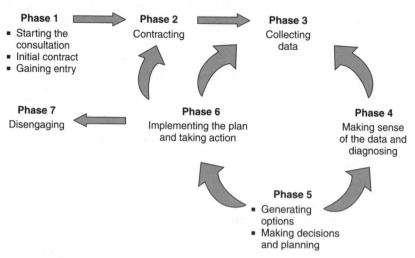

Figure 5.1   Consultancy cycle

discussions about the project are still critical in terms of setting expectations and establishing relationships. Creating early impressions and 'Getting in' with your client were discussed in Chapter 4, as was the need to market yourself, even if you have a monopoly position.

Phase 2 – Making and maintaining effective contracts with your clients

This phase is critically important and will be discussed in more detail later. It refers to setting contracts in terms of what, how, where, when and who. This will include being able to analyse the stakeholders with a vested interest in the work; contracting with them as necessary and engaging them throughout as appropriate.

Phase 3 – Skills and tools to collect information about a presenting issue

This might include the ability to design questionnaires and interview people effectively. Good observation, listening, questioning and analytical skills will also be needed at this stage. Familiarity with diagnostic tools may also be critical if you are gathering data at a more strategic level.

Phase 4 – Diagnostic skills

This phase entails making sense of the information in the context of what else is happening in the organisation, or part of the organisation, within which you are working. This stage requires a good understanding of organisational development and organisational and group dynamics, plus the ability to stand back and interpret what is really going on in any given situation, so political awareness is useful here.

Phase 5 – Generating and selecting options

In this phase, you need to be able to work with your clients to decide the most appropriate course of action. This could include a training intervention; recommendations about systems, structures or processes which need to be changed; recruitment and retention strategies or other interventions aimed at improving the business and/or people's experience in the workplace. This stage will require good presentation and influencing skills, plus political skill and sensitivity.

Phase 6 – Implementing the recommendations

The skills needed here very much depend on the intervention. Facilitation and change management skills as well as some expert knowledge are likely to be needed.

Phase 7 – The ability to disengage effectively

This phase refers to knowing when you are helping and when you need to hand over the process to your client. The ability to disengage effectively is a skill in itself and is explored in more detail in Chapter 9.

Many of the underpinning skills in this model will be familiar to HR professionals – such as the ability to question, listen, develop rapport, facilitate discussions and present information. Whilst not straightforward, developing these skills is covered comprehensively in other publications, and it is not the intention to go over these here. Some of the other skills mentioned, such as positioning yourself with your client, influencing change, political aptitude and disengaging are covered in other chapters of this book. Consequently, this chapter focuses primarily on the importance of Phase 2 of this model, which is the ability to contract effectively with clients.

However, projects are rarely as neatly presented as a consultancy cycle. As a Business Partner, you may get brought into a project at the implementation stage in the role of a pair of hands. If you have concerns about what you are being asked to do, then the ability to challenge and backtrack through the cycle will be a critical skill for maintaining your credibility. One Business Partner commented that 'being presented with the solution which someone thinks is right to implement, rather than being allowed to research the issue/problem and complete a full consultancy process' was one of the most challenging aspects of her role.

Benefits of Internal Consulting

Whilst this model applies equally to internal and external consultants, Lacey (1995) points out that there are advantages and disadvantages which come from having an internal perspective, some of which are outlined in Table 5.1.

The Diagnostic phase of the consultancy cycle, for example, can provide challenges for both the internal and the external consultants.

Table 5.1 Advantages and disadvantages of being an Internal Consultant

Advantages	Disadvantages
Phase 1: Gaining entry	
Familiar relationships	Must work with everyone
Little marketing required	Cannot drop a project
Steady pay	Less prestige than externals
Less conflict of interest	Work may be boring/routine
Familiarity with jargon	
Phase 2: Contracting	
Ease of verbal contracts	Informality may lead to lack of clarity
Knows the systems and players	Juggling demands of changing confidentiality and openness
Phase 3 and 4: Collecting data and diagnosing	
Knows where to look for dysfunction	Can be part of the problem
Moves freely in the organisation	May not have the latest techniques
Can involve the right people	Client retaliation or dependency
Understands the culture	Prestige determined by job level
	Change anxiety in consultant
Phase 5 and 6: Selecting options and implementation	
Knows the 'fit' of options proposed	May have limited vision
Identifies the key power sources	Free and informed choice is unlikely
Ensures proper follow-through on ideas	Project failure may humiliate
Phase 7: Disengaging and evaluating	
Success may be linked to status	Failure may lead to loss of status
Success broadens opportunities	May experience alienation/ isolation from clientsystem
Gets to see long-term impact	May get little recognition for themselves

Lacey (1995, p. 83), reprinted with permission from Emerald Group Publishing Ltd

On the face of it, the Internal Consultant should more easily be able to access information in the organisation through either primary or secondary methods. However, sometimes the role of someone working internally can be viewed with suspicion and so access to certain individuals or information may prove difficult if full trust has not been established. A positive advantage for the Internal Consultant can be an ability to identify with the culture and values of the organisation and how they impact on behaviour. A skilled consultant will be able to identify how they are impacted by what is happening in the organisation as a member of that system and use themselves as a live part of the diagnosis. For example, if communication of change is leading to confusion and anxiety in the organisation, the Internal Consultant is also likely to experience this. If they are able to stand back and assess what they are experiencing, this can be another valuable source of data contributing to the overall picture of what is happening.

Those working internally will have to deal with their own feelings of discomfort and anxiety about the changes before they can effectively support others – working to uncover dissonance in their own value systems before working with others. The Internal Consultant can easily find that clients become overly dependent on them as experts. Managing client anxieties as someone working internally, with their own fears and concerns about change and how this might impact on them, can also result in unhelpfully co-dependent relationships. It will be really important for the Internal Consultant to demonstrate the behaviours they are trying to influence in others when selecting methods for data gathering and diagnosis. In this way they will be able to build credibility and respect by 'walking the talk'. Issues of confidentiality are also key during this process. External consultants are more likely to be trusted to respect confidences and act impartially, so the Internal Consultant needs sometimes to work harder at demonstrating a commitment to keeping confidences.

As an internal consultant, Business Partners would benefit from reviewing this list and thinking through how they can counter some of the potential disadvantages. Some Business Partners, for example, will bring in external consultants to work with them if they feel they are too close and immersed in the problem they are working on.

The Importance of Contracting

> *Consultants naively imagine that contracting is a short, straightforward business deal and not the complex social–political interaction that it is.*
> (Jean Neumann, *Developing organisational consultancy*, 1997)

At first glance, contracting with your client appears to be a straightforward task. There are a number of different elements that need to be discussed, debated and agreed at the start of any project, and once this has happened the end outcome is usually documented in some way to provide evidence of the discussion and clarity about how you will work together. However, as you dig deeper into what makes a successful Business Partnership between HR and the line, it becomes increasingly clear that the effectiveness of each stage of the process, from initial data gathering through to implementation, is dependant on the quality of the contracting meetings with the client and that if these discussions are not thorough enough, many misunderstandings or unrealistic expectations can occur as a project develops.

According to Roffey Park Research (Kenton and Moody, 2003), only 6.9 per cent of companies include contracting in their top three competencies for Internal Consultants. Yet having a clear contract with the key decision-makers is critically important when working as an Internal Consultant, perhaps more so if working internally where the boundaries of the relationship can be less clear. It seems that those working internally are often faced with competing priorities and this, combined with a lack of perceived power and influence, can mean it is a challenge to define the boundaries and priorities for work presented by clients.

Contracting on an internal basis tends to take place in an informal way and with little attention to defining the time and other resources which might be needed for the work (including access to people). Whilst there are constraints to having a too tightly defined contract which leaves little flexibility, some defined parameters can be extremely useful for helping establish roles and responsibilities for both the consultant and the client.

As well as a focus on the 'what' of contracting, exploring the different elements of a project, Business Partners also need to examine the 'how' in terms of establishing how the relationship with the client will operate.

Whilst it is easy to get drawn into a discussion on the issues presented by the client, it is equally important to discuss early on how consultant and client will work together in order to lead into an exploration of the consultant role.

Do I even need to contract?

Business Partners who work predominantly for one client, or for whom the role is less tangible than project delivery, may feel that there is less of a need to contract with their client. Whilst specific projects may require scoping and clear terms of reference, ongoing process interventions may be harder to tie down, or the way of working with the client may be very established. Many organisations, such as *Severn Trent Water*, used their Business Plan as Terms of Reference for the work of the Business Partners, as this provides clear goals, timescales and deliverables. However, as one Business Partner described it, 'my work is like a bottomless pit and I need to prioritise and manage expectations constantly. Holding contracting discussions is a way of achieving this.' We would echo these words and suggest that contracting on the less tangible aspects of the role is often *more* critical than the key deliverables.

Contracting with your client and setting terms of reference for a particular project, or elements of your role, has a whole range of benefits:

- It can help the client to develop their thinking about an issue and work out what they really need from you, rather than what they first think they need
- It leads to a mutual understanding of the 'what' and the 'how' behind the contract
- Jointly exploring a problem will help you to establish a better understanding of the business issues and background to the issues
- It provides an opportunity for you to redefine your role from one of a support function to that of an equal partner
- Clear terms of reference provide a benchmark for assessing the effectiveness of your performance.

However, even when the benefits are evident, it can still be hard to tie down a client as an internal provider. *Airbus* aim to agree a charter with their clients to prevent constant change to the project brief, but admitted that there was resistance to being tied down by the client system.

Who should you contract with?

The consultants in the Roffey Park research (Kenton and Moody, 2003) identified a difficulty in establishing exactly *who* the client is and some even cited 'the whole organisation'. In a sense it is often true that the client is the organisation and this makes it even more important to identify key members of the client group in order to gain access to the more senior levels and decision-makers in the organisation, which can often be difficult. One Internal Consultant from *The Body Shop* stated that they 'spent time getting clear client relationships – recognising that in every piece of work there is likely to be more than one client – users, deciders, influencers etc' (Inside Outreach Ltd, 2002).

This issue of who is the real client becomes even more difficult to establish when the Business Partner has dual reporting lines. Determining whether a project is being driven by the HR business or the Operational business may not be that easy to assess and as a consequence loyalties may well come into play. One way to help with this is to establish success measures which are agreed with both reporting lines as a way of clarifying which client agenda you are following.

Even when the Business Partner is clear about who the client is, it can sometimes become apparent during contracting meetings that the client does not really own the problem and that the true owner is elsewhere in the organisation. If this occurs, it is important to question whether the issue should be re-contracted closer to the source of the issue if at all possible, as this will help to provide the level of commitment required to make any recommendations effective.

The sponsorship role

It is also important to consider the other stakeholders in the client system, such as any suppliers, consumers or sponsors. Part 1 examined the role of sponsors and other stakeholders in the organisation. A sponsor for the piece of work may or may not be identified by the client, but where the Business Partner is involved in helping with an aspect of change, it will be important that they are not seen as the 'champion' of the work. If this occurs, the Business Partner may become the scapegoat if the change does not go as per plan, or feel an increasing need to justify their position. Rather, it might be more appropriate if sponsorship comes at the most senior level of the organisation.

In discussions with consultants it seems that there is little exploration in the contracting stage about the role and responsibilities of the sponsor. This may mean the role becomes more of a token gesture than a committed and valued contribution. Contracting needs to include consultant expectations of the sponsor. This is a potentially difficult conversation for those working internally. Useful questions to ask might be:

- What would effective sponsorship look like?
- How would this be demonstrated so that people throughout the organisation know the work has commitment and backing at the most senior levels?
- Would multiple sponsors be appropriate for this project?

Nortel ensure that they appoint 'sustaining sponsors' as part of their steering committee for new projects (Morris, 1996). The role they have defined for these sponsors is to:

- Remove political and organisational impediments
- Seize opportunities to champion the project
- Help market and sell it to other leaders
- Give advice on politics to the team
- Keep the team motivated to achieve
- Hold the team accountable for meeting milestones.

The role is clearly defined as a leading and active position, rather than just a spokesperson. *The Hyde Group* also renamed their sponsors 'saviours' to reflect their championing role.

What to Do at the Initial Client Meetings

When you first meet the client, or hold an initial meeting with them by phone, the client will be making almost instantaneous impressions about you. Having gained entry, the next step is to hold a more in-depth discussion with the client on a particular issue or project. Whilst there is usually a need to negotiate a formal agreement for any piece of work, equally important in these initial client meetings are the aspects that focus on the psychological or unspoken contract which is being established between the Business Partner and the client.

Before we go on to discuss the practicalities of contracting skills for Business Partners, it may help to include a short paragraph about content, procedure and process and how we are defining these terms here.

Content, procedure and process in an organisational context
Content – in an organisational system will include the overt policies, structures, business plans and strategies. The task-focused things that are in place make explicit what we are here to do. It can also be the explicit agenda at a meeting.

Procedure – will be the 'how' we go about doing the business. It will include processes and systems in place, the methods by which we get things done. The meeting in itself is an example of procedure – it is the method we choose to get something agreed or discussed. Other methods might include training, telephone conferencing, workshops, interviews, etc.

Process – includes the things below the surface in the classic iceberg model; the beliefs and assumptions that people carry, the preconceived ideas, the gossip and grapevine, the shadow system that can either help the organisation achieve its goal or get in the way. In our meeting example, some of the process will be visible around non-verbal body language – the asides, doodling, tone of voice, etc.

The Business Partner needs to be able to determine at which level interventions are needed and what else needs to happen to support change. For example, in an organisational context, if an appraisal system is changed at a content level, how will this impact on the way appraisals are carried out? What needs to happen to pay attention to the procedure? And what might be the underlying feelings of the appraisers and of those being appraised? (process).

Content and process between individuals and groups
Here, content is about the words people use. The language chosen can give you an important indication of what else is going on at an individual level. For example is your client saying 'we' and meaning 'I'? This may mean the client wants to disagree with what you are saying but does not want a confrontation, so pulling others into the conversation can be a way of feeling safe. Are they putting their

'buts' in your face! – I remember hearing Marshall Rosenberg, founder of Nonviolent Communication (NVC), speaking at a recent conference about the aggressive use of the word 'but'. Usually, the use of this word will mean that someone is feeling defensive or not listening to what you want to say (Rosenberg, 2003). By paying attention to your own words and those used by the client you may be able to make the communication clearer.

The tone of voice and non-verbal behaviour is the 'process' of the conversation, otherwise known as the music and the dance behind the words. The tone of voice someone uses can give invaluable clues as to how they feel about a suggestion or a piece of feedback, for example. Mixed messages tend to arise when someone says one thing, but their voice or facial expression gives you a contradictory message. You might choose to reflect this back to your client by saying 'you don't seem to be sure' or 'you're looking a little puzzled about what I've just said'. The aim again would be to clarify the communication between you.

Noting content and process at an organisational and individual level can help to extend our choice of interventions. It will not always be appropriate to pick up on process explicitly, but it can help to aid our understanding of what is really happening.

Formal contracting issues
The more formal part of the contracting process is content based and entails discussing and debating a number of issues and drawing up a contract, or initial terms of reference, based on what is agreed. A good contract is likely to:

1. Agree objectives and the overall scope of the work
   - What type of outcome is expected – a change, a solution or recommendations?
   - What does success look like?
   - What is the purpose of the project?
   - Who are the people involved?
   - What are the boundaries of the work?

2. Set timescales and plan the phases of work
   - Is it fixed or open-ended?
   - Whose time will be needed at each stage?

- What are the key deliverables?
- When will they be delivered?
- What are the key milestones?

3. Agree who has responsibility for each aspect of work
   - Who is the sponsor and what is their role?
   - Who is in a steering role for the diagnosis and design?
   - Who has decision-making capability?

4. Agree data gathering methods and access issues
   - What methods are appropriate for the project?
   - What methods suit the context?
   - Who can you talk to?
   - Who and what must you avoid?

5. Agree how the work will be communicated
   - Frequency of contact
   - Method of communication
   - Confidentiality agreements.

6. Outline the finances and any financial implications
   - Which budget is it coming from?
   - Who can authorise payments?
   - Are there penalties for late delivery?

7. Detail other resource allocations
   - Staffing
   - Materials/Equipment.

8. Outline any dependencies and risks that may affect the intended outcomes
   - What assumptions are being made?

9. Establish a review process and a process for re-negotiation
   - How will the project end?
   - Will any ongoing support be required after completion?
   - How will the project be reviewed?

- What methods of evaluation are appropriate?
- Who will instigate re-negotiation of the contract if there are changes?

Each of these elements is essential in the contracting process as problems can easily arise if they are omitted. Attempting to spend two or three days carrying out a thorough evaluation of a project at the end of the process, for example, is almost impossible if this was not discussed and agreed up front.

Many of the items on the list also require a skilled conversation to get to the root of what is required and how the contract will be carried out. Confidentiality, for example, is an important issue which is often raised but seldom explored in sufficient depth. Cockman et al. (1992) suggest that an effective discussion on confidentiality will cover:

- What confidentiality means with respect to the issue?
- Whether data gathering will be collected and reported openly?
- How the findings will be distributed?
- Whether access to the data will be given for other purposes?
- What levels of involvement are appropriate?

This list alone, however, is fairly formidable as an agenda for a meeting, so it is important not only to prioritise the key elements so that they are discussed and clarified as soon as possible, but to also flag up any items which do not get covered and ensure you gain agreement to come back to them at a future meeting. Often the initial contracting process can take several meetings, depending on the complexity of the project. For highly complex projects, Gantt charts are often used as a project planning tool.

How formal do you need to be?

In some organisations there is a need within the existing process to formalise and sign off an agreement for every project. This may seem overly formal in small companies and the contract does not necessarily need to be the type of document that requires joint signatories. A detailed e-mail may be sufficient if this suits the culture and management style of the organisation. However, even in companies where it is not common practice to formalise verbal agreements, it can still be very useful for the

Business Partner to summarise the contents of a contracting meeting and send this to the client to check that there is a common understanding of the points raised.

The informal contract

Much of the discussion at the initial meetings with the client is likely to focus on the issue they are seeking to address. The Business Partner will be using their skills to probe the client about the nature of the problem in order to help gain clarity on the task at hand and establish the formal contract. Mixed in with this, discussions may also take place on the informal contract, such as the role expectations (expert, pair of hands, collaborative, etc.) and how the client and Partner would ideally like to work together.

As if that was not enough, there will also be a whole host of non-verbalised perceptions taking place at a process level, such as:

- Do I really want to work with this person?
- Do I trust them?
- Do I like them?
- How competent do I think they are?
- Do I agree with what they are saying?
- How knowledgeable are they?
- Do I feel a sense of rapport?
- Do their questions make me think?

From a Business Partner perspective there are a number of mini-agendas which are worth holding in the back of your mind during the initial set of meetings with a client.

What is the bigger picture?

Useful information at this stage is to get a sense of the department, its objectives and customers as well as how the issue fits into that and what has already been tried and with what outcome. Background information such as why the client has chosen you (if they had an option) may also be useful.

It is important for the Business Partner to check out any assumptions about how the problem is defined and any possible solutions that are raised. Often a client will have made some preliminary diagnosis about their particular situation and may be resistant to suggestions that more data needs to be gathered before devising a solution. The Business Partner needs to try to retain an open mind on the likely reasons for the problem occurring and continually encourage the client to question their assumptions and take a wider view of the possible options.

Where does the power lie?

It is important to get an understanding of who has the power to make which decisions in relation to the assignment. Getting an understanding of the key stakeholders and who needs to be involved in the process of decision-making can be essential if you are to avoid treading on people's toes and wasting a lot of time tailoring the project to the wrong people.

Exploring what you are prevented from doing with the client can be a useful way of finding out some of the power politics occurring. Are there certain things that you can only talk about to certain people, for example? Getting a good understanding of the organisational relationships and how these help or hinder the situation is vital information and is often one of the key advantages that Business Partners have over external consultants.

What are the potential underlying problems?

The 'presenting problem' which the Internal Consultant is asked to tackle is often complicated by the overlaying culture of the organisation. For example, a request for a team-building event may, on further diagnosis, show that a controlling leadership style or unfair reward strategies are the main contributors towards dysfunctional team behaviour. Internal Consultants can find it difficult to get permission to go behind the presenting issue and get to the root cause of problems – often due to the issues of role, status and power highlighted above. Effective contracting plays an important part here in clarifying the expectations of both the consultant and the client.

What are my needs and expectations from them?

It may be important for you to convey certain information about yourself or the way you like to work to your client and gain commitment to this. For example, you may have particular biases which you would like them to acknowledge. Peter Block (2000) recommends making a list of essential and desirable needs which you can then hold in your head when entering into a client discussion. Possible needs include:

Essential needs	Client support for a particular approach
	Establishing co-operation for data gathering
	Commitment to the project by the client
Desirable needs	Open and honest feedback
	Tolerance of mistakes
	A share of the credit if all goes as per plan

If your essential needs are not met, or there is a mismatch between your values and those of your client, you need to consider whether it is possible to turn down the work. Internal Consultants in the Roffey Park research identified difficulties in 'saying no' to work even when it did not seem to be of high priority. The culture of the organisation will have a significant impact on the consultant's ability to set priorities and manage the boundaries of their work as well as the expectations of their role.

What are their needs and expectations of me?
As well as overtly discussing what a client needs from you as a partner and how they expect you to work with them, a Business Partner also needs to be constantly on the look out during the initial meetings for the subconscious cues stemming from the client. Often consultants will say that they have discussed their role with their client and that the client has agreed that they would like to work collaboratively with the Business Partner. This is not surprising as this can often sound like the right thing to say. However, if a Business Partner is able to pick up on the nuances of the client's body language, they will be aware of any confusions or insincerities and explore these further. It can be more fruitful to start from a point of asking what expertise the client is looking for, which will bring out collaborative skills if these are required.

Responding appropriately to the client's emotions can often be a challenge. Business Partners often try to rescue the client rather than remaining neutral in the situation. Table 5.2 illustrates some of the possible emotions that might be exhibited by a client during an initial meeting. For each emotion there is likely to be an emotional reaction which is triggered, but the skill of the Business Partner lies in being able to respond in a neutral way.

Table 5.2 Partner responses to client emotions

Emotion	Neutral reaction	Emotional reaction
Confusion	Clarify issues	Get sucked into the confusion
	Clarify roles	
	Provide a structure	Oversimplify
	Restrain action	Fight
	Assess the impact	Take sides
	Provide models/maps	Accept one frame of reference
Conflict	Learn its history	Fear it
	Welcome it and understand it	Minimise it
	Value the differences	Ignore it
	Provide an arena	Take sides
	Model conflict handling	
Worry/fear	Listen	Teach
	Acknowledge feelings	Falsely reassure
	Explore sources and nature	Contract unrealistically
Stuck	Establish what they have	Do it for them
	Find out what worked before	Work with solved problems
	Find out what hasn't worked	Solve symptoms
	Start where they are	Suggest your favourite solution
	Establish needs and wants	
	Provide relevant input	

Adapted from Clarkson and Kellner (1995, p. 12) with permission from AMED

A client will also have needs and expectations about how they want you to behave towards them and how much commitment they expect from you. Once again, the more you can draw these thoughts into an open discussion the more clarity you will have.

Will I have the level of access to people and resources I need to be effective?

During the contracting discussions Business Partners are often faced with a dilemma as to whether to work within the constraints on offer, or to negotiate for what they ideally need. For example, your client would like you to find out about a particular aspect of work but is not prepared for you to question some of the key stakeholders or ask particular questions. This is a difficult judgement to make, as the Partner is often balancing the need to appear helpful and flexible towards the client against a need to work in the most effective way. However, effective Partners will challenge and explore the resources on offer before deciding how far to push. Ultimately, if a Partner takes on an assignment without the permission they need to access adequate resources or people, their credibility is likely to suffer more than if they advise the client up front that a particular course of action will not work in the way proposed.

Gauging success

At the end of the discussion, if it has gone well there will be a greater sense of commitment between the client and the Business Partner, and the trust and respect between the parties will have grown. A quick test of the success of a contracting meeting is whether the Business Partner has managed to bring out all the anxieties of both parties and gained a clear commitment of how to proceed.

Avoiding Some of the Pitfalls of Contracting

Perceiving contracting to be an upfront activity

Whilst the majority of the issues for any assignment will need to be clarified and agreed early on in a project, it would be wrong for a Business Partner to assume that once they have a written agreement there is no more contracting to be done. Each review period, project milestone or emerging issue is an opportunity to revisit some of the initial assumptions that were made with the client and re-negotiate the contract if appropriate. The client contract should be a live agreement that is continually challenged and amended as appropriate.

Having said that contracting should be an ongoing activity, there is also a danger in this, in that the client may use it as an opportunity for continued re-negotiation of the contract and the ground rules. Steps also need to be taken therefore to set expectations up front about the nature of any re-contracting that might take place. In addition, the Business Partner needs to be prepared to challenge their client if they feel they are being taken advantage of.

Straying too far into data gathering

In trying to establish the underlying problem being presented by the client, it is easy for a Business Partner to risk straying into an unplanned phase of data gathering. Whilst this might not be a problem, it can lead to difficulties if it either gets in the way of other aspects of the contracting which should be taking place, or leads to assumptions being made on how to progress the project without a more accurate diagnostic study. One of the key skills of the Business Partner is being able to gather enough data on the issue to be able to draw up an initial contract, without getting too drawn into the work to be able to take a step back.

Starting to carry out work before a contract is agreed

It may seem obvious that work should not begin on a particular project until the contracting issues have been discussed and agreed, but often there is a pressure to begin the work beforehand. It may be, for example, that a key stakeholder is only available for interview the next day, or that a particular department needs a key deliverable on a set date. Whilst this is not quite critical if there are no cost or fee issues involved in the Partnership, it is still equally important that the contract is fully discussed before work commences. Without this happening, misunderstandings are likely to occur, expectations will not be met and it will become increasingly difficult to revisit some of the initial conversations which still need to take place.

Acting unprofessionally

It is particularly critical in the early stages of a project that you make every attempt to convey a respectful, open and honest manner towards your client. Over-familiarity with a client, or a sense of inferiority compared to the client can lead to the Business Partner acting unprofessionally.

Key guidelines for dealing professionally are:

- Arrive on time
- Be clear and open about your objectives
- Acknowledge your client's opinions and respect their values
- Be honest about the limitations of your work
- Challenge your client if you do not understand anything they are saying

- Actively listen and appreciate your client's position
- Be prepared to admit any misunderstandings on your part
- Avoid giving personal opinions on people in the organisation
- Provide your client with choice as to how to proceed.

Things to avoid are:

- Talking more than listening
- Not managing the time during the meeting
- Voicing recommendations too soon
- Appearing inflexible in your approach
- Leaving the meeting without a clear agreement on next steps.

It can be useful, particularly if you are working as part of a larger Partnership group, to document client meetings. If someone needs to pick up on your work or follow-up in your absence then the Partnership can be seen to act far more professionally. Figure 5.2 shows an example of a meeting report form.

Ignoring a lack of commitment from the client
Sometimes a Business Partner will come away from a meeting with a feeling that the real issues or anxieties were not openly discussed. This can occur when the Business Partner is enthusiastic and confident about a piece of work and the client is not totally committed to what is being discussed, or it may just be that the client is very trusting of the Partner and abdicates some or all of the responsibility for the issue without the necessary willingness to participate in the discussions.

One of the key skills of effective Business Partners is that they will raise concerns they may have and, even when they are not clear where the concerns originate, will be prepared to say so and explore this with the client. Whilst Business Partners can potentially be effective at instigating organisational change without a strong client commitment, their effectiveness and perceived success will be greatly enhanced by ensuring that they gain commitment up front.

Sometimes a client may just have a low motivation either for the project in hand, or for a full contracting discussion of the type described. One reason for this may be that they do not see the value in the process and need to be helped to do this. Another possibility may

---

Meeting Report Form

Date   24 January 2005

Location   Glasgow Office

People present   PG, AW, ST

Objective of meeting   To get an understanding of the client issues
                              concerning turnover.

Background/Structural information
Turnover currently at 35 per cent in the call centre. Previous year was
26 per cent.
Currently six call centre teams of ten, each with a team leader.

Issues arising
Newer recruits are turning over faster – possibly due to fewer opportunities
for promotion to team leader – possibly due to graduates working before
getting a 'proper' job.
   Induction training is good, but existing staff feel a bit neglected.

Suggestions made
Talked about exit interviews for leaving staff; morale of current staff;
change to IT processes; Team Leader skills; competition in the area.
   Discussed need to do more analysis of the possible underlying causes
before making recommendations.

Actions
AW to come back in two weeks to propose a way of gathering more data
to diagnose the cause.

Figure 5.2   An example of a meeting record

be that they do see a value, but their priorities are not in your favour!
In these cases, taking small steps and contracting on each stage at a
time may be a better way forward or, alternatively, negotiating with
your client to work with another person from the client system on the
contracting issues.

Reaching an impasse
It is easy to reach an impasse in your initial discussions with a client, as it
will be the first time they have thoroughly explained their needs and

expectations and you have raised yours. If these needs and expectations do not match, which typically occurs in areas such as required timescales for delivery, then you may hear yourself repeating your points over and over again, or your client may continue to state their position and be unable to move on. You are likely to feel a sense of irritation at this point, but the blocks may not always be evident, as the language used is often coded. For example:

The client says	'Why don't you think it over and get back to me?'
The client means	I want you to do it the way I'm suggesting.
The client says	'Let's gather some more evidence.'
The client means	I don't agree so you can prove it if you like.
The client says	'Right' or nothing at all.
The client means	I'm confused and don't really understand what you're saying.

It is important to recognise that you have reached a blocking point before you can move on from it. Ways forward include:

- Revisiting your own needs and expectations to see if they are realistic.
- Pointing out the impasse to the client and getting agreement to put it to one side and move on.
- Thinking creatively with your client about how to get around the different needs.

Closing the contracting meeting

It is useful to allow some time at the end of your initial client meetings to summarise all that has been agreed and take time to review the process. Asking how the client felt about the meeting, the project and you as a Business Partner may be difficult questions to pose, but will be invaluable in launching you into an open and honest relationship.

Summary

Consultancy Skills are an essential part of a Business Partner's toolkit. The ability to establish yourself with your client and contract effectively are critical building blocks to your success. In addition to the key skills which underpin the consultancy model, such as questioning, listening and building rapport, there are higher-level skills involving political influence, awareness of process issues and ability to diagnose.

This chapter focused predominantly on contracting, which is a key component of the consultancy cycle and is not just about establishing the parameters of a piece of work. Done well, it is about having some difficult conversations with people in the organisation about roles, responsibilities and expectations. It takes guts for a more junior Business Partner to have an honest conversation with a senior sponsor about what they need them to contribute rather than just accepting them as a figurehead for a project.

Due to the vast number of issues which require clarity at the start of any project, contracting is not something that can be tied up in one meeting with the client. The formal elements of the contract alone can take some time, and it is also important to raise and deal with the intangible process elements. Effective contracting provides a thorough basis for a continued relationship with your client and provides greater assurity that your work will be focused appropriately and valued by the client and the organisation.

Checklist

- Have you got a good understanding of the consultancy cycle?
- Are you taking steps to minimise the disadvantages of consulting internally?
- Are you clear you are contracting with the right client?
- Have all the tangible elements of the contract been agreed?
  - Objectives and scope of work
  - Timescales and milestones
  - Responsibilities
  - Data gathering issues (including access)
  - Communication
  - Resources: finance, staffing, facilities, etc.
  - Dependencies and risks
  - Review and evaluation procedure
  - Process for re-negotiation.

- Have you developed a sense of the potential underlying problems to what is being presented?
- Do you have a clear sense of the surrounding issues?
- Have you gained sufficient data to be able to progress?
- Have you left the way open to revisit the contract?
- Have you clarified roles and expectations for both yourself and the client?
- Have you challenged and explored any emotional responses stemming from the client?
- Have you acted professionally throughout the process?
- Have you raised any reservations you have about the contract?

References

Block, P. (2000) *Flawless Consulting*, 2nd Edition, Jossey-Bass/Pfeiffer, San Francisco.

Clarkson, P. and Kellner, K. (1995) 'Danger, Confusion, Conflict and Deficit: A Framework for Prioritising Organisational Interventions', *Organisations and People*, Vol. 2, No. 4, pp. 6–13.

Cockman, P., Evans, B. and Reynolds, P. (1992) *Client-centred Consulting: A Practical Guide for Internal Advisers and Trainers*, McGraw-Hill, Maidenhead.

Inside Outreach Ltd (2002) see www.inside-outreach.co.uk.

Kenton, B. and Moody, D. (2003) *The Role of the Internal Consultant*, Roffey Park Institute, Horsham.

Lacey, M. Y. (1995) 'Internal Consulting: Perspectives on the Process of Planned Change', *Journal of Organisational Change Management*, Vol. 8, No. 3, pp. 75–84.

Lippit, G. and Lippit, R. (1986) *The Consultancy Process in Action*, 2nd Edition, Jossey-Bass/Pfeiffer, San Francisco.

Morris, D. (1996) 'Using Competency Development Tools as a Strategy for Change in Human Resource Function: A Case Study', *Human Resource Management*, Vol. 35, No. 1, pp. 35–51.

Neumann, J. E., Kellner, K. and Dawson-Shepherd, A. (1997) *Developing Organisational Consultancy*, Routledge, London.

Rosenberg, M. B. (2003) *Nonviolent Communication: A Language of Life*, Puddledancer Press, Encinitas CA.

6

Understanding Self in the Context of the Organisation

For organisations to survive and thrive when change and uncertainty are prevalent, there is an increasing need for Internal Consultants to go beyond the fundamentals and build their capacity to really understand themselves in the context of the organisation.

More advanced consultancy skills are key to really working alongside managers and helping them to understand and work with the organisational issues that challenge them.

If we look at the consultancy cycle, at one level it seems a straightforward process; however, in reality things are often more complex. If we take contracting for example, we may think we have agreed a contract with our clients which is about providing a management development programme for all middle to senior managers to help them improve their ability to motivate and develop their staff. We have agreed the expected outcomes with our client and we may expect to have access to the senior management population as a way of ensuring that the changes that are needed are made effectively. However, unless this has been made explicit in the contracting stage, we may find our attempts to engage and work with the senior managers thwarted. Contracting is just one stage of the cycle that needs a more in-depth understanding and awareness to be able to really carry it out effectively.

So What are the More Advanced Skills?

To be really effective in the consultancy role, however that is defined, we need to be able to be critically reflective in our practice. More recent organisational change models highlight the importance of continual environmental scanning, so that the organisation is adaptable and ready for change (Stacey, 1996). In the same way, consultants need to be continually able to tune in to their own practice; reflect and evaluate what they are doing in the moment and match that to what is happening outside the group, organisation or other systems in which they are working. It is also about the ability to draw together underpinning theory and knowledge and apply this, together with a heightened self-awareness, in day-to-day practice.

At the top of the model in Figure 6.1, 'reflective practice' is shown as the end result of a number of other key aspects of advanced consulting. Let us discuss each of these in turn.

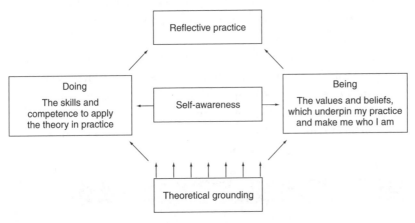

Figure 6.1 Reflective practice
Source: Kenton (2004)

Theoretical Underpinning

As most, if not all, people applying consultancy skills within an organisational context will be facilitating change at some level, certain underpinning theory will be helpful to understand. The following are some examples of theoretical underpinning that might be helpful for Business Partners:

- *Organisational development and culture* – models of culture, systems theory and thinking, models of OD
- *Organisational design* – models of organisational design, business process mapping, designing organisational structures, aligning strategy and structure
- *Organisational and group dynamics* – stages of group development, team roles and preferences, theories of conflict and behaviour, psychodynamic theory
- *Change theory* – transition curve, linear and complex change, emergent and chaotic models, large-scale interventions for rapid change
- *Business strategy* – links to HR strategy, business process management, business performance measurement
- *Quality systems*
- *Research methods* – including quantitative and qualitative research, grounded theory, action research
- *Learning and development methods* – what they are and how they can be applied – in what contexts – coaching, mentoring, shadowing, action learning and projects (for example).

At a more advanced level of consulting, the practitioner will need to go beyond understanding the theories and be able to judge what they mean in the context in which they are working; drawing on relevant theory in the moment and, where appropriate, bringing this awareness into conversations with the client. We do not intend to go into all these theories in more depth in this book.

Awareness of Self, Others and the System as a Whole

We all have a level of self-awareness which helps us to exist in the world. I am aware that I am hungry and I eat (although even some of these basic levels of awareness are becoming underdeveloped). For those of us in roles that involve helping other people and organisations, our level of self-awareness needs to be more acute. 'Getting our own house in order' is an expression which is often used in relation to the helping professions and while most of us might not be professional counsellors, there will still be a requirement to deal with some of the 'messiness' that goes with organisational and personal change interventions. It is important for those of us working as consultants and/or using consultancy skills to be aware of the interventions that we make and the likely impact on others. This includes how we behave from moment to moment and our personal process as well as the more content-driven processes and interventions that we might make. A fictitious example here might help to elaborate on this point:

> *Debbie is a Business Partner at Performican. She has been called in at short notice to a meeting with Mr Jones, one of the senior managers, and is feeling a bit flustered about what he may want. Shortly after arriving in his office it is clear that he expects her to come up with some expert suggestions about how to increase low morale in his team, which has escalated to the point of someone walking out that morning. Debbie knows the individual and is concerned and anxious about how he may feel and the impact on the other team members but feels unable to say this. Instead, under the pressure of time and Mr Jones's insistence that she 'sorts something out quickly', Debbie finds herself promising to facilitate a meeting with the team that afternoon.*

This example raises some of important points about self-awareness as a key part of the advanced consultancy skills set:

■ Knowing and paying attention to any ingrained patterns of behaviour that we might have. For example, drivers such as 'please me' or 'try hard' (Berne, 1966)
■ Paying attention to our ability to keep grounded in challenging situations
■ Paying attention to our needs and emotions from moment to moment
■ Recognising what is happening in the here and now and how we are reacting on both an emotional and a behavioural level
■ Being able to self-evaluate the effectiveness of our reactions and responses
■ Knowing what our strengths, hooks, triggers and limitations are
■ Knowing when our overall health and well-being needs attention.

If we are self-aware then even if our behaviour is in some way inappropriate, given the situation, it can be rectified. So Debbie, in the example above, may have been aware of how she was feeling about the situation in Mr Jones's team and consciously decided not to disclose that. Facilitation of the team meeting might be a useful intervention, if Debbie is consciously choosing to do this on the basis of self-awareness, rather than as a reaction to Mr Jones's insistence that something is done quickly.

Self-awareness can be thought of as part of our *Being* and *Doing*. *Doing* is about our competencies to fulfil our role; having the skills set to carry this out and the tools and techniques to be effective.

Debbie, in the example above, has a CIPD qualification and good facilitation skills; she is accredited to use psychometric instruments and has built up good knowledge and skills in facilitating change over a period of 10 years. She has the skills to coach individuals and experience in facilitating numerous events for managers and teams in challenging change situations. This knowledge and skills set make up the *doing* part of what makes Debbie effective. Her self-awareness will let her know where her strengths are on the *doing* side and where she might need further development.

Being is more about the energy we bring, our personality, our integrity and ability to relate to the client at some human level. So this is about who Debbie fundamentally is as a person; her values, beliefs and sense of self. This side can be strongly developed as in a healthy plant; like an early shoot that needs some attention, or even an unfertilised seed. Being clear about our values and beliefs can strengthen our capacity to work congruently with our clients. Debbie may want to re-check some of her beliefs in working with managers in the organisation and consider the implications of these. For example, if she believes:

- The more senior the manager the more respect they need to be given
- Her role is to provide the service as specified by the manager
- That she must have all the answers all of the time
- That doing something is better than doing nothing
- That the manager's needs are more important than the members of his team
- That she should never say no.

The list is not definitive! You can see how these beliefs may lead to ineffective behaviour in this situation. However, Debbie may have a healthy, strong and supportive set of beliefs which are then not played out in her behaviour. This mismatch can lead to incongruence. Therefore, Business Partners applying consultancy skills well will be able to identify when their behaviour is congruent with their beliefs and the values of the organisation and when they are not.

Reflective Practice

> *So what then is reflective practice and how does it link to the advanced consultancy skills set?*

Schön (1983) challenges the conventional view of professional practice in that practitioners need to draw not only on their technical knowledge and specialist skills, but also on tacit knowledge and understanding which he calls 'knowing-in-action' – learning how to re-frame difficult problems into situations which can be helped. This is more about the art of consultancy than the science. This capacity to reflect, both in day-to-day practice and as part of our continuous development is, according to *Schön*, the key to professional practice.

If Debbie in our earlier example had the ability to reflect well, a number of things might have happened. Her reflection in the moment may have highlighted how she was feeling about the situation, and she may have decided to disclose her own reactions to the news of the recently departed team member. By role modelling congruence in this way, Debbie may allow the manager to get in touch with his own feelings about what has happened.

By reflecting after the event, Debbie may have pondered on how Mr Jones was acting and made links to both her experience of him in other situations and her knowledge and understanding of people and how they react in change situations. For example, Mr Jones may have been quite shocked at the sudden departure of one of his team members and projected the blame on to Debbie. Her understanding of group dynamics may have given her some insights into how the team were responding to a relatively new boss and other changes that had taken place recently. By being able to reflect both in the moment and afterwards, Debbie's choices of interventions are immediately increased.

Part of the advanced skills set is the ability to bring our reflections on what is really going on into conversations appropriately.

The Use of Power in Organisations

To understand the organisation, its culture and ways of working, we also need to consider the question of power – what it is, who has got it, how they use it and how to draw on power to help us achieve our objectives. Power does not have to mean domination, rather it can be thought of as energy, or drive, to achieve goals.

Power bases

Power in an organisation can be used constructively or destructively. The uncontrolled use of power in an organisation can mean that people achieve their goals at the expense of others or the organisation overall. We all need enough power to enable us to get things done, and a first step is recognising what power we have.

There are many sources of power that people have in organisations – often without realising it. It is important not to overlook the power of the stationery clerk, for example, or the finance manager. One reason to consider power bases is that you have an idea about what power the people you want to influence have. Another is to consider for yourselves which of the following you already have and which you could usefully increase towards greater organisational influence. Examples of power bases follow:

- *Resources* – to give out or to take away resources such as people, money and equipment
- *Information* – access to information which might be useful to others in the organisation
- *Specialist knowledge* – this could be on a range of topics, for example reward strategies, quality management tools, etc.
- *Status/authority* – this might link to position but could also be job title or role
- *Position* – in an hierarchical organisation, the higher up in the organisation, the more power someone will tend to have
- *Reward* – to be able to reward people by, for example, giving them a good appraisal, or a pay rise, or the ability to take these away
- *Reputation* – being able to command respect based on previous deeds
- *Interpersonal* – using good interpersonal skills to create impact and respect

- *Personal* – a sense of self-worth which creates personal presence in the company of others
- *Political* – a good understanding of the informal networks, how these work and how to use them to influence others.

Which of the above do you have now? And which could you build on? Which are valued most highly in your organisation?

In our experience the sources of power which have either remained constant, or are on the increase, are interpersonal, personal and political. In the knowledge age, specialist knowledge and information will often have credit too. Status/authority and positional power tend to be on the decrease in organisations that are flatter for a quicker response to change.

Understanding the politics

As well as thinking about the sources of power that you and your internal clients will be operating from, an understanding of the organisational politics will be key to influencing successfully.

Politics with a small 'p' within an organisation can still have negative connotations. We often come across individuals who are working in an internal consultancy role who would prefer not to engage with the organisational politics. However, it may depend on whether you view political activity as neutral, negative or positive. Linda Holbeche's research on political activity in organisations draws on data from 120 professionals across Directors/senior managers and middle managers (one focus group consisted of HR professionals) (Holbeche, 2002).

In the research, respondents rated political behaviour in the following ways:

- Using strategies to achieve personal goals at the expense of others/the organisation (27%)
- Using strategies to achieve personal goals irrespective of the impact on others/the organisation (33%)
- Using strategies to achieve personal goals which also benefit others and/or the organisation (40%).

Interestingly, in the last category women respondents outnumbered men (25% to 16%).

Some of the other findings from the research are shown below:

- 65 per cent of respondents agreed that political behaviour is part of natural human behaviour
- Men were slightly more inclined to see politics as natural human behaviour (38%, with women at 27%)
- 63 per cent of survey respondents agreed with the statement 'people engage in political behaviour as a defence mechanism'
- 87 per cent of respondents felt that political behaviour was most likely to occur in large organisations
- 49 per cent thought organisational politics was on the increase, 44 per cent said they thought it was about the same over the last three years, and 7 per cent felt there was less politics.

What does it mean to be political and to have political skills?

This links closely for us to questions of ethics for Business Partners, which are discussed in more detail in Chapter 7. However, it will certainly include having an understanding of the informal networks and the culture of the organisation and using that knowledge and understanding in a way that best serves the business and the individuals within it.

Kim James and Simon Baddeley (1987) developed a four-part model to highlight different aspects of political understanding and behaviour (Figure 6.2). These include the ability to 'read' and understand the political environment and 'carry' certain political behaviours into situations. The levels of awareness are shown from 'politically unaware' to 'politically aware' and the behaviours and skills from 'psychological game-playing' to 'acting with integrity'. The skills shown on the left-hand side of the model tend to be more focused on achieving personal goals at the expense of others and those on the right-hand side on behaviour which has the organisational needs in mind.

Business Partners will need to be skilled at both understanding the political environment and acting in a way which best serves the organisation and individuals within it. The model can also help in developing our awareness of others' behaviour and how best to respond, particularly with individuals you want or need to influence.

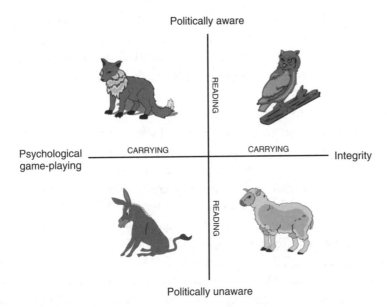

Figure 6.2 Descriptive model of political behaviour
Source: Reproduced from James and Baddeley (1987) with permission from AMED

What it means to be an innocent sheep?

When individuals come into an organisation they may be unwittingly act-ing as 'innocent sheep' in that there is a sense of naivety about how things really work in the organisation. So if the policy says all annual leave needs to be agreed by the senior manager, the assumption may be that that is the reality. The innocent sheep may find in practice that leave is taken on a 'first come first serve' basis and they miss out on taking leave at their preferred time. By sticking to the rules and acting on principles, the innocent sheep is at risk of being attacked or gobbled up by the fox!

Possible actions for supporting the innocent sheep
It does not necessarily pay for the organisation to have too many people in this category, partly because it is more about maintaining the status quo than engaging with the change process. Some ideas on developing the innocent sheep include:

■ Having a good induction scheme which talks about the values and culture of the organisation as well as the overt rules and policies

- Having a buddy system, so that individuals can draw on the experience of others to find their way around the informal systems
- Training programmes which cover political skills and influencing
- Offering a mentor – using some of the wise owls in the organisation.

What it means to be an inept donkey?

The inept donkey according to the James and Baddeley model describes someone who is still politically unaware, but through their own self-interest engages in psychological game-playing. This term comes from Transactional Analysis (Berne, 1966) and demonstrates how people get their needs met at a psychological level, through their interactions with others. The donkey then is someone who is emotionally illiterate and uses unprincipled and unethical interventions to get noticed and increase their influence.

However, because this is done in a somewhat clumsy way, you may notice a lack of tact and diplomacy here. Examples would include disclosing unhelpful gossip in an inappropriate environment, the proverbial 'putting one's foot in it'.

Possible actions for supporting inept donkeys

You may feel that donkey behaviour needs to be ignored or put down as it certainly seems to be an unhelpful and possibly destructive set of behaviours. However, it is difficult to really be clear about the intention of using this behaviour, without knowing the individual concerned. If for example, we believe that everyone's behaviour has a positive intention for that person – that is, they have a basic need which gets met by their behaviour at some level, we might approach it differently. Certainly left to their own devices, people behaving in this way can cause an annoyance at best and provoke conflict and tension amongst others at worst. Here are some options for dealing with donkey behaviour:

- Pick up on any underlying message – for example: 'Are you really saying that all the support staff are below performance?'
- Pick up on any underlying feelings – for example: 'You sound angry about being left out of that decision.'
- Give direct feedback – for example: 'I feel uncomfortable about you talking about George when he isn't here and would prefer you talk to him directly.'

- Ask questions to find out what their needs are, for example, to be more directly involved in things or for greater social contact.
- Involve them more – it may be that showing some trust is just what they need.

What it means to be a clever fox?

When we include a session around organisational politics in any of our programmes at Roffey Park, the behaviour that most people recognise most strongly is that of clever fox. This set of behaviours includes the ability to read the organisational politics and use it to one's own advantage. It differs from the inept donkey in that it is a much more subtle set of behaviours and skills. It could include someone who is in a post for a short period of time and gets their objectives met, but at the expense of others around them. The fall-out from this behaviour is not always seen until after the event, if at all. There is a charming veneer which disguises the intention in a way which makes it difficult to spot. This individual can recognise the power bases and use them well, exploiting weaknesses to meet their end goal. Sometimes in organisations this behaviour is seen as valid and is actively encouraged and valued. It often will mean short-term goals are met, as with other aggressive behaviour strategies. However, the long-term implications are usually serious. It can create an environment where people are 'watching their backs' and levels of trust and openness are low.

Possible actions for dealing with the clever fox

Here, more than with the other behaviours, you may well be questioning the need to support the clever fox, although the same question applies to the fox as to the donkey: 'What needs are not being met, which results in expressing behaviour in this way?' As a first step you might try some of the strategies mentioned for the inept donkey. However, you could spend a lot of time and energy trying to understand the behaviour, when what you may need to do is limit the damage done by the clever fox. As a first question it will be important to be clear about the behaviour and whether it really is clever fox or wise owl. Your reading of the situation will be key to this. Is the behaviour fundamentally serving the purpose of meeting the individual's needs at the expense of others and/or the organisation? If you are not sure, you may want to check out some of your assumptions before jumping to conclusions. Some suggested actions for dealing with clever fox behaviour are shown below:

- Use your observation and listening skills to really hear and understand the behaviour.
- Check out any assumptions by asking questions of those who might be impacted by the behaviour – for example: 'How did Jo's decision affect you/your team?' Try to remain neutral.
- Find out where their allies and enemies are and get to know them – what is their experience of this person.
- Use some of the skills referred to for dealing with donkey behaviour – pick up on the process as well as content of what is being said but be careful about how you do this and in what company!
- Support others who might need help in dealing with the behaviour. Use your coaching skills.
- Chunk up important decisions which will impact on other teams or the organisation more widely. At meetings, bring these wider issues to the attention of the group. For example – 'How will this affect the finance people and our longer-term strategy?'
- Choose methods for your projects which include a wider range of diverse people, so that it is not just the clever foxes who get to say how things should move forward.

What it means to be a wise owl?
We should say at this stage that rather than seeming to label everyone else's behaviour around these descriptions, in our view, we can all be behaving in some of these ways at any time. This is more about being attuned to the behaviours that are displayed by individuals in organisations including ourselves and giving consideration to some of the choices we may have about how we deal with them. Wise owl behaviour in the model is about understanding the political terrain and acting with integrity. The wise owl has not only the interests of others at heart, but also the interests of the organisation. They are interpersonally skilled and politically sensitive. In our view, this does not mean being totally open all the time. Rather, it is about paying attention to what is going on between different people and groups in the organisation; understanding the nature of the business and what needs to happen to get the business needs met

and using their sources of power in a way which supports others rather than subjugates them.

*Using wise owls in the organisation and developing more wise
owl behaviour*

Fortunately, many people we have worked with also recognise the wise owl behaviour in their organisations. These tend to be the people who have earned respect and credibility and are both approachable and diplomatic. It should be stressed here that these are not necessarily people who are at the most senior level of the organisation. They do, however, recognise their own sources of power and use these to help others and the organisation overall.

- Use wise owls to mentor others in the organisation.
- Get them involved in championing specific projects and influencing others in the organisation.
- Use them as a role model – notice what they do and how they do it, if you want to develop more of these skills for yourself.
- Ask for their views at important meetings if they are not being expressed and get the organisational take from them to widen others' perspectives.
- Is there anyone amongst the wise owls who would be a good mentor or coach for you?
- Develop your own political awareness. Talk to people in the organisation about its history and listen to stories about how things are done around here.
- Keep in mind the first, second, third and fourth perceptual positions, to make sure you are paying attention to the wider needs.
- Get feedback on how you are perceived in terms of your political skills and sensitivity. This could be either by way of a 360-degree feedback or more informally from people you trust and know will be honest.

Networking

Ask anyone who works as an external consultant about the importance of networking, and they will be quick to confirm that their success will be in part as a result of the networks they have built. A lot of time and effort will often be put into networking by external consultants. Attention also needs to be given to this by those working inside the organisation. Having a good network of people both within and outside the organisation can help to raise your visibility and credibility. Pay attention to who you network with. You will need to be aware of those who may have hidden agendas and could use you for their own advantage.

A little like the term 'organisational politics', networking can be something which is not looked upon with too much relish. Here are some assumptions that you may have about networking:

- It is manipulative
- It is more of a selling job than anything else
- People will think I am pushy
- It seems false
- People will think I have got nothing better to do
- It is about small talk and I have not got time for that
- It is all about small talk and managers have not got time for that.

We need to examine some of these in more detail. If you have any negative assumptions about networking, here are some other ways to look at it:

It is manipulative

What does manipulation mean anyway? One dictionary definition is to 'handle or control with dexterity' which does not sound too bad to us. What people usually feel uncomfortable about is any approach which is in some way underhanded. Networking really is more about letting others get to know you and what you can offer them. After all, they may really want your service and want to get to know how you can work with them to support their business needs.

It is more of a selling job than anything else

Part of networking is about selling – selling yourself and your role. However, if you are confident that you have the knowledge and skills that are needed by the business in order for it to be more successful, you can be confident that others will want to use you to help them too. It is also more than just selling, it is about showing a genuine interest in others and the roles and challenges they face in their day-to-day work.

People will think I am pushy

People may well think you are pushy if you are! If you are perceived to be pushy it may be that you are approaching networking as an aggressive activity rather than assertively seeing it as a 'win–win' opportunity. Pay attention to timing; if the people you want to network with are really too busy to see you, you may want to wait until there is a better opportunity. Look for ways that you can support them with challenges they are currently facing; find out what is going on in their area of the business and then offer support as a way of getting to know them better.

It seems false

If you are genuine in your approach and intention then you will be perceived to be genuine. Consider what you can offer others in the organisation as well as what they can offer you. Think of it as part of what being a professional service provider is about.

People will think I have got nothing better to do

Another way to think about this is that people may think you are genuinely interested to find out what is happening with them and in their area of the business. Many people will see these conversations as you doing your job, getting your face known and taking an interest in their issues. It is important not just to turn up when there are problems but to get to know people when things are going well too. Letting managers know that they are doing okay and giving positive feedback when things are working well is as important as supporting them when things go wrong. Also, time spent in getting to know the senior managers is crucial to ensure that you have strong links when you need support on projects.

It is about small talk and I have not got time for that

It is important to make time. It is part of the role of the Business Partner, and the wider your network the more contacts you will be able to draw on – not just to help yourself but to help others in the organisation too. Develop your 'resource investigator' (Belbin, 1993).

It is all about small talk and managers have not got time for that

Not all managers will want to spend time engaging in small talk and you need to be sensitive to that. However, showing a genuine interest tends to be appreciated by most people. It does not have to be time-consuming; it could be as simple as saying 'how are you?' and really listening for the answer. The first step is convincing yourself that you have something to offer.

So What is Networking?

Networking is essentially the ability to build and maintain credibility by creating and maintaining effective relationships and exchanging relevant information. For the Internal Consultant or Business Partner this ability and skill is essential, not just in terms of maintaining your own credibility but also in terms of enhancing other people's under-standing and awareness within the business. Your ability to help others network too will be invaluable in helping the organisation to share knowledge and move further towards a learning organisation.

The networking skills listed in Table 6.1 will help you to self-assess and consider where you might increase your potential in this area.

Table 6.1 Networking skills

Networking skill/behaviour	Doing it well now	Some improvement needed
■ A genuine interest in other people	☐	☐
■ Understanding of the business and issues facing the organisation	☐	☐
■ Understanding of the culture and 'way things are done around here'	☐	☐
■ Good listening skills	☐	☐
■ Aware of your own body language and its impact on other people	☐	☐
■ Ability to ask pertinent questions	☐	☐
■ Sharing knowledge and information with others	☐	☐

Table 6.1 Networking skills—Cont'd

Networking skill/behaviour	Doing it well now	Some improvement needed
■ Willing to disclose your understanding of the culture of the organisation	☐	☐
■ Able to read body language and what is really being said	☐	☐
■ Sensitive and tactful when dealing with others	☐	☐
■ Ability to remember people on a personal as well as professional level	☐	☐
■ Able to engage in small talk	☐	☐
■ Proactive in meetings and getting to know those who are new to the organisation	☐	☐
■ Getting back to people when promised on an issue	☐	☐
■ Good at showing appreciation of others	☐	☐
■ Facilitating introductions of other people	☐	☐
■ Easy and approachable style of communication	☐	☐
■ Letting people know how to contact you	☐	☐

How Else Can the Skills be Developed?

- ■ Building your competence
- ■ Clarifying your values and beliefs set
- ■ Knowing your limits
- ■ Looking after yourself

- Paying attention to the politics
- Building emotional awareness and resilience
- Getting support
- Committing to continuous professional development.

Building your competence

What knowledge, skills and attitudes do you need to carry out your role? A fundamental part of being effective is to have some clarity about role purpose. Even if the individual parts of your role change and you want to be responsive to emerging needs and trends, having some clarity about what you are fundamentally in the organisation for and what you are expected to achieve will help to provide a sense of being grounded in the organisational context. For example, Debbie (in our earlier example) has a role purpose 'to provide strategic advice, support and challenge to the business towards improved organisational success'. From this as a basis, she can then work out what the knowledge skills and attitudes will be towards that end purpose. A whole host of activities might then contribute towards Debbie's personal development plan.

Margaret Struder, Regional HR Manager of *Cargill Europe*, identified some key ways in which her HR Business Partners are being developed, including moving people to different countries to get cross-country experience and broaden their understanding of cultural differences; giving people real responsibility in the Business Units to stretch them sufficiently, for example around acquisitions; visiting sites, such as in Germany, to get closer to the customers and assigning a coach or mentor outside their direct area.

Clarifying your values and beliefs set

This one is a little trickier, but you might start by writing down your answers to some key statements:

- Organisations provide opportunities for . . .
- The role of the Business Partner is . . .
- The role of the senior management/Executive team is . . .
- Managers at all levels in the organisation need to . . .
- People are engaged in the business best by . . .
- Employees have a responsibility to . . .

- It would be unhelpful for someone in my role to . . .
- My priority in this role is to . . .
- I believe change is . . .
- Decisions in this organisation need to . . .

You can build up your own list of questions to help you get closer to identifying what you believe and what your values are around your role.

Knowing your limits

This links to self-awareness. It is important to recognise our personal and specialist limitations in providing a service to others. You know, for example, that if someone wants you to give them advice about finance or budgeting which is *not* your area of competence, then you should not attempt to provide that advice.

Equally, you might have spent the last three weeks delivering challenging developmental programmes and you know that any more time in the training room would not be helpful for you or for the group. Be prepared to say no to work that is beyond your present capability. Alternatively, get help and support if you view the work as an important part of building your own competence.

The role of the Business Partner is becoming increasingly complex and wide. Agreeing some boundaries for the role will help to prevent becoming over-stretched and the dangers of under-performance.

Looking after yourself

Ask yourself from time to time – what would balance in my life mean? And work towards achieving that aim. Balance means different things to different people but by paying some attention to spending quality time both with family and friends and at work, you are more likely to be productive and grounded in your practice. Looking after yourself also means paying attention to health and well-being including getting emotional needs met.

Paying attention to the politics

Get to know the internal politics. Build your networks and use your influencing skills to have greater impact, and also to build your understanding of how the organisation works and the dynamics within it.

Building emotional awareness and resilience

Take appropriate risks by stretching your own comfort levels from time to time. This might be done by taking on more challenging work or by asking directly for feedback from clients. By using self-disclosure and feedback, you will be able to increase your awareness of self and others. Keeping a learning diary is another way to pay better attention to how you are experiencing what is happening around you. Resilience may come from internal reflection or from talking to others. Try to maintain a healthy balance between seeking support from others and positive self-talk. Meditation can be another useful way to ground our experiences and build resilience.

Getting support

In any role where you are supporting others – building and maintaining support networks for yourself will be an important aspect of your ability to remain effective. This might include spending some time talking with colleagues in your immediate work environment; having an internal or external coach or mentor; being able to discuss work issues with a supportive partner or family member (although beware here that you are not offloading too much on to one individual); belonging to appropriate professional networks; and regular and planned meetings with colleagues in a similar role. The use of learning sets or support and challenge groups can also be extremely helpful to maintain effective practice.

Committing to continuous professional development

In our view, no-one should be in a supportive profession without making a commitment to continuous professional development. How you do this will be very much up to you – it might include training programmes, coaching, mentoring, reading, writing articles, attending network meetings, etc. The list of possibilities here is quite long. Make sure that some of the development focuses on you getting to know you better.

Summary

Key skills for Business Partners and Internal Consultants will include organisational and business awareness; influencing and political skills; excellent interpersonal skills; specialist HR skills; and consultancy and change management skills. Above all, though, the ability to understand the organisation as a system and develop the skills of a reflective practitioner will be key to success in the role. Developing your understanding of how organisations and systems work, together with an ability to reflect on your practice both in the moment and between actions, will help you to make more informed choices about how you work with your clients and within the organisation.

In certain professions such as law and medicine, practitioners are required to commit to a number of days per year for their continuous professional development. While this is not the case at the moment for Business Partners, we recommend that you build in time to develop your own practice each year. Working with others in a supportive capacity means you are offering them expertise and advice which needs to be kept up to date. Having some clarity about what is happening in the wider business world, your own particular niche and your organisation in particular will help inform your work and the advice you offer to others. Knowing the self and developing your self-awareness and resilience will also help you to be a more grounded practitioner.

Checklist

- What are you doing right now to develop your self-awareness and awareness of others?
- Have you established regular links with other Business Partners/ Internal Consultants in the organisation to discuss how your work links with theirs?
- Have you established a personal development plan for yourself towards continual professional development?
- What reading/research are you doing to update your knowledge and skills on how organisations and systems work?
- Have you targeted specific individuals who can help you understand the organisation or parts of it better?
- Have you established a good support network?
- Are you taking time for reflection each day?
- Have you got at least one project which stretches you at the moment?
- Have you got too many and, if so, what are you doing to limit the number of these?

- Are your feedback systems in place and working?
- Have you clarified your job purpose?
- Are you clear about the boundaries of your role?
- What strategies have you got in place for influencing change? And how do you know if they are working?
- Which sources of power are you actively engaged in building?

References

Belbin, M. (1993) *Team Roles at Work*, Butterworth-Heinemann, Oxford.

Berne, E. (1966) *The Games People Play*, Penguin, London.

Holbeche, L. (2002) '*Politics in Organisations*', in Conjunction with Director Magazine, Roffey Park Institute, Horsham.

James, K. and Baddeley, S. (1987) 'Owl, Fox, Donkey or Sheep: Political Skills for Managers', *Management Education and Development*, Vol. 18, Pt 1, 1987, pp. 3–19.

Kenton, B. (2004) 'Advanced Consultancy Skills', *Training Journal*, October.

Schön, D. (1983) *The Reflective Practitioner: How Professionals Think in Action*, Maraca Temple Smith, London.

Stacey, R. D. (1996) *Complexity and Creativity in Organisations*, Berret-Koehler Publishers Inc., San Francisco.

7

Relationship Skills

For us it comes down to 3 things – Relationships, Relationships, Relationships
and through these enabling our clients to do so much more for themselves.
Jean Floodgate, The Body Shop International

It is almost impossible to describe the numerous immeasurable factors
that go into creating an effective relationship between a Business
Partner and their client. However, it is clear that before you can even
begin to build a sound relationship with a new client you need to
develop good rapport and empathy with them. Once you have a good
rapport, you need to start to build your own credibility as a Business
Partner and operate within a set of values that show integrity and
professionalism. As if that is not enough, effective Business Partners
also need to be able to deal with the pressures and conflicts that are
likely to emerge during the course of a project. Business pressures as
well as political pressures from within organisations are part of everyday life, and the ability of Business Partners to deal effectively with
these pressures is critical in sustaining an effective role.

Developing Rapport and Empathy with Your Client

Understand the client's perspective
Clients like to feel comfortable with the person they are dealing with
and one way to build and sustain rapport with your client is to identify
common interests or values. If rapport does not come easily to the
relationship, then showing a genuine interest and understanding of the
issues and constraints facing the client can go a long way. The Business

Partner needs to put themselves in the client's shoes and gain a real understanding of the client's personal and business goals from their partner's perspective.

Be genuine

There is a strong temptation when faced with a client to adapt your style and suggestions to suit what the client is explicitly asking for and the way they operate. This is particularly the case when there is a perception that the Business Partner's credibility stems from demonstrating their expertise and that their added value comes from providing lots of ideas and answers to questions. Ineffective Business Partners who follow this approach will soon find that they are putting forward suggestions and ideas that they themselves are unsure of. Whilst it is true that Business Partners do need to draw on some expertise, Partners who have a mindset that it is the client who adds the value (as they hold the real key to the problem or the situation) find it much easier to show a genuine interest in the client's issues and work with their agenda to help move the project forward. The evidence suggests that the people who clients continue to use are those who think about and are genuinely interested in what the client's needs are and how to address them, rather than continually suggesting their own preferred approach. Business Partners should still use their own expertise, knowledge and ideas, but need to tailor them to the context of the client.

Go beyond the expressed needs

Developing rapport requires the Business Partner to empathise with the client and understand not just the words being said but their thoughts, emotions and interests as well. A truly collaborative approach is rarely reached by working only on the expressed needs of the client. Valued relationships between clients and Business Partners operate at a deeper level, where both have professional as well as personal trust in each other.

There is a need to listen to what is *meant* rather than what is *said* by the client. This entails picking up on clues in the client's body language and emotions and reflecting back your interpretation. For example, when a client says 'That might work' this could either mean the client really does believe it will work, or that there is a small possibility, or that it is unlikely to work for them. Partners need to sense any lack of conviction in the client and ask questions to draw out the true meaning behind the words. In this case, the Business Partner might say, 'I am getting the feeling that you are not really sure it will work – tell me why that is.' Given that only about 7–10 per cent of the impact of communication comes from the words that are used, tuning into the non-verbal cues and the tone of voice is essential. It is not possible to overstate the importance of active listening, paraphrasing and checking understanding as key skills for an effective Business Partner. Effective Partners are likely to do twice as much listening as talking.

Understand the whole person

To gain empathy Business Partners need a real understanding of their clients on a number of different levels.

- *Character*: How do they operate? What are their preferred ways of working?
- *Perspectives*: How do they see the future? What do they see as the company's position?
- *Motivation*: What is their interest in the project? How important is it to them? What really motivates them in their role?
- *Values*: What principles drive the way they operate?
- *Understanding of the pressures on the client at that moment*:
  - The political situation
  - Their relationship with their peers
  - Their relationship with their seniors
  - The marketplace
  - Their satisfaction with work
  - Factors affecting them in their home life
  - Their hot spots.

Understand your own biases

In order to be sure of your own biases, it is useful to have a clear understanding of your own personality type as a Business Partner. People tend to ask questions within their own frame of reference and when we hear something we attempt to evaluate it, rationalise it and make an interpretation in a way that makes sense to our own models of behaviour. The more you have an understanding of what your own filters are, the easier it is to suspend judgement for a longer period and seek to expand your own frame of reference to allow an increased number of possibilities. As an example, a Business Partner may have a bias towards team-building activities as a way of improving relationships within teams. It may be that they have had a lot of success with this method in the past. However, it may be that the situation presented has an underlying problem that would make team building less effective on this occasion, and jumping too early into discussing possible solutions will limit the Partner's ability to understand the complexity of the situation and reach a more effective resolution. The less quick you are to judge as a Business Partner, the more likely it is that you will reach an optimal solution.

Establishing and Maintaining Trust

Developing rapport and empathy with your client is the first stepping-stone in building their trust (Figure 7.1). How you choose to operate and act beyond this will determine whether you can sustain your position and build trust and credibility.

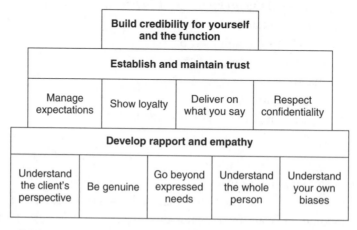

Figure 7.1 The building blocks to trusting relationships

Manage expectations

People buy from people and a client will continue to use you only if you establish trust. However, trust can easily be destroyed and is particularly impacted by taking risks which may backfire. Without encouraging some risk-taking however, it is unlikely that the Business Partner will be adding significant value to the business. So, what is important is that the Partner manages the client's expectations when faced with a risky situation. Face-to-face time with the client is essential not only in providing an opportunity to set and manage expectations, but also in helping to increase the level of rapport and empathy. Pfau and Cundiff (2002) argue that one of the key factors in establishing trust is for the Business Partner to help stakeholders understand the strategic human-capital issues facing their organisation and to explain the rationale behind change-related decisions. Only in this way will the client group understand what the Business Partner is trying to achieve.

Show loyalty

Loyalty is an important part of trust. If your client always comes second or third on your list of priorities, they are likely to sense this and will feel that you cannot be trusted. Partners can demonstrate loyalty by putting the client's agenda first.

Deliver on what you say you are going to deliver on

Trust is usually broken by not following through on actions or letting your client down in some way. This may sound straightforward, but the quickest way to lose both trust and credibility is to not to do what you have committed to up front. Even if there are perfectly valid reasons why something is not happening as planned, it is important that this is communicated effectively to *all* involved, or you risk damaging your reputation. Trust is broken very quickly and a client may not explicitly tell you that they are unhappy. The first indication that trust is broken is likely to be a slight change in behaviour towards you and a sense that there is a vague dissatisfaction which is not being aired. Regaining trust is hard work and it is much better to admit mistakes or inability to follow through on promises before the client finds out.

Respect confidentiality

With an effective partnership, confidentiality issues are addressed up front and it is clear who has access to what and which conversations are open and which are not. This is not always easy to sustain as an internal Business Partner. Often you will be asked for other people's views or for your own perceptions of individuals or situations and it is not always clear how open you should be. It is important to avoid criticising others or being indiscreet if you want to maintain a sense of trustworthiness. Coupled with this is a need for Business Partners to have a strong sense of what their own principles are, so that when they are faced with difficult situations it is immediately clear which path to follow.

Building Credibility

Credibility takes place both for the Partnership Function as a whole, in terms of its marketing and perceived value, and at an individual level. Table 7.1 illustrates the key factors in establishing credibility for both aspects.

Table 7.1 Key determinants of credibility

Individual credibility	Functional credibility
■ Work on the client's agenda	■ Increase visibility
■ Establish some quick wins	■ Understand the business
■ Be proactive in providing information	■ Use appropriate procedures
■ Use your expertise appropriately	■ Gain relevant qualifications
■ Have conviction in what you say and do	■ Pull in expertise from outside when it is needed
■ Work only in areas that add value	■ Stay in touch with the market
■ Do not get emotionally drawn in	
■ Always get buy-in to the solution	
■ Be responsive	
■ Present messages carefully	

Individual Credibility

Work with the client on their agenda

Credibility comes from working with the client on their agenda rather than your own. To be truly credible you need to get a real understanding of where the client is in relation to the project and use listening, empathising and questioning techniques to great effect in order to draw the links between what is being said and the bigger picture.

Establish some quick wins

Individual credibility is built primarily from positive feedback from significant players in the organisation. When first starting out, 'quick wins' are useful for establishing a reputation for delivering change. 'Clients for Life' (Sheth and Sobel, 2000) and 'The Trusted Advisor' (Maister et al., 2002) describe how Business Partners always need to start from the position of being a hired expert and that the first step in building a longer-term relationship is to move to become a steady supplier (Figure 7.2).

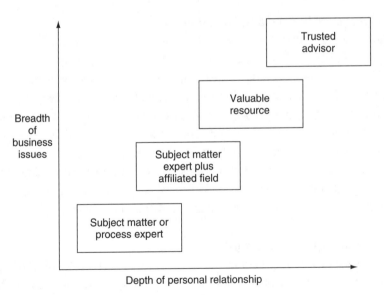

Figure 7.2   Evolution of a client–advisor relationship
Source: Drawn from Maister et al. (2002)

This move comes from showing reliability in what you do and doing what is expected. Once you are a steady supplier for a particular client, then you can strive to the position of 'trusted advisor', where the Business Partner can add real value by working collaboratively with the client to help provide real insights. They argue that you cannot expect to start a relationship in a truly collaborative way.

However, despite this being a natural development of the role, there are dangers if the quick wins are not utilising the whole range of partnership skills. An Internal Consultant from *HBOS* described to us how, during the restructuring of the *Royal Bank of Scotland*, they had been primarily used in a purchase–sale role and were attempting to re-position their Business Partnership as more of a process role. However, they found that you soon get a reputation for delivering in a certain role and that it is then difficult to break the mould. They managed to find a way round this by getting in on the early stages of strategy discussions, before the diagnosis began. This does serve as a word of warning, however, that if your quick wins are based on effective implementation and delivery of projects it may not be as easy to develop into a Partnership role and that quick wins carrying out effective diagnosis or design may be a more useful starting place.

Be proactive in providing information

Anticipating information which may be useful to your client can provide a real opportunity to gain unexpected praise or positive feedback. Clients are often too busy to keep on top of all the management information which may be useful to them, and unexpectedly being presented with something pertinent to their issues can be very powerful in leveraging your credibility. Having the client's agenda in mind when going about other things may lead you to picking up on thoughts, ideas or written documentation which is of use to their project. Surprising your client with information they have not asked for can be very useful in building your relationship as well as benefiting the business.

Use your expertise appropriately

If you are positioning yourself as an expert in a particular aspect of the project, it is important that you do have this expertise. You need to be honest about what you know and what you do not or the client group will see through you.

There is a difficult balance between credibility and expertise. If you ask a client what they value in a Business Partner, it is not often that they state expert knowledge at the top of the list. More often the ability to trigger thoughts and ideas in the client is the skill that is most valued. If Business Partners continue to provide sound expertise without building a strong relationship then it is likely that eventually the client will go elsewhere to buy the same expertise at a cheaper price.

Have conviction in what you say and do

Although Business Partners often have concerns that a decision is not based on sufficient data or that it appears based more on intuition than fact, if you believe in a particular course of action then credibility can come through pursuing the approach with conviction. The beliefs and passions of Business Partners can help to create an energy which influences the client system and helps to move a project forward when people have doubts.

Work in areas that add value

In order to be seen as credible, Business Partners may need to turn away work when it is not appropriate. Working as an Internal Consultant may mean that you get asked to do work that is helpful for your client, but does not add value to the business. Often there is a pressure on internals to help out in these situations, but doing this on a long-term basis will damage both your credibility and your perceived value.

There may also be occasions where there is work that will add value, but you do not have the time or resources to take on the task and give it your full attention. Much as you would like to work on a particular project or with a particular client, doing so at this time would leave you overstretched and consequently ineffective as a Business Partner. Effective Partners will be assertive with their clients when these issues emerge and will be honest about the situation.

Do not get emotionally drawn in

If a project or situation is interesting it is likely there will be conflicting views emerging and this may lead to heightened emotions. It is critical that Partners remain calm and levelheaded about the situation in order to take a more rational view. Conveying energy and interest is important, but emotional involvement will restrict your ability to see the bigger picture. In order to do this, individuals need to have a clear sense of their own emotions and biases and put these to one side. Having said this, it is also important that Business Partners pay attention to what their own emotions may be telling them and use these feelings to raise any concerns or ideas that they may have.

Get buy-in to the solution

If you are working effectively as a partnership then the client will have worked with you to develop a solution. However, not all clients have the time or interest to devote to projects and you may find yourself working in a harmonious way with a great deal of delegated authority. Whilst it may be clear to both you and the client that the decision on what will happen is down to you, it is still essential that you deliver what is expected by the client. It is imperative that you take the time to explain your intentions and rationale as early in the process as possible, in order to ensure the client gains some ownership for the solution. You sometimes need to educate your client in order for them to understand your value.

Be responsive

A client needs to be able to count on you to do what you say you are going to do. Partners need to be both consistent and reliable, as a client wants to know where they stand and what they can expect from you. Business Partners need to be responsive in a number of aspects:

- *Timings*: Being flexible with scheduling to suit the client's needs as well as ensuring that all the milestones are met.
- *Needs*: Ensuring that all their needs are met by the solution.
- *Budget*: Ensuring that the diagnostic work and recommendations can be achieved within the budget.
- *Other departments*: Your main client should be your priority but your reputation will also come from being responsive to others within the client system, so it is also important that you remain responsive to others.
- *Accessibility*: Make sure you can be reached or that people can leave messages for you. It can be very frustrating for a client not to talk to you when they need to and it is good practice to respond to client questions and calls as quickly as you can, even if it is just to say you need more time to formulate an informed response.

Be careful about how messages are presented

Often people will ask you to 'tell it straight', but in reality will be sensitive to feedback they are linked with in any way. Clients can easily get defensive or take things personally and it is not uncommon for the Business Partner to be used as a scapegoat. Effective Partners need to be very tactful about how information is presented. A good approach is to invest as much time working on how to communicate and on the engagement strategy as the activity itself.

Credibility for the Function

Understanding the business is a fundamental part of building credibility for the function. In addition, the following will help to improve your image.

Ensure there is visibility in the organisation

The Business Partnership Function needs to be visible in the organisation and provide a clear sense of the type of work that is being undertaken and the value that the Partnership brings to the company. Newsletters, brochures, involvement in organisational events, etc. with success stories and feedback from projects can all add to this. High-level sponsorship for projects can also be vital in drawing attention to the work taking place.

Establish appropriate procedures

The Institute of Management Consultants (IMC) has a code of conduct which principally covers:

- Meeting the client's requirements
- Integrity
- Independence and objectivity.

It may be appropriate for the internal partnership group to use these as a basis for an organisationally tailored code of conduct, which would have the added benefit of raising some of the less-talked-about issues of confidentiality and ethics to the fore.

Other aspects which may require more consistent approaches are setting clear terms of reference and contracting for each project; and communication between Business Partners and feedback processes. Project management disciplines are often used to structure the process throughout an assignment.

Gain appropriate qualifications

Where Business Partners need specific expertise, they need to ensure that they have appropriate qualifications. For example, it may be that an HR Business Partner needs to be licensed to deliver particular psychometric tools.

Pulling in expertise

Neumann (1997) highlights the relationship with external consultants as key to the success of internal Business Partners. He argues that the more effective partnerships will build good relationships with external consultants and are more prepared to draw in their expertise when it is missing internally. This can also be used as a learning opportunity for the internal partners, if they choose to work alongside the external partners, although it needs to be carefully managed to ensure that perceptions of credibility are not damaged.

Stay in touch with the market

Keep a strong network of contacts inside the organisation and outside. Good Business Partners need to keep up to date with changes in the company and the section therefore needs a process for collecting relevant company literature and information on the business and market changes.

Dealing Effectively with Pressures along the Way

Even when Business Partners have a good rapport with their clients and have established a strong sense of credibility and trust, there are still likely to be pressures impacting on the relationship that could limit its effectiveness. Some of these pressures will stem from the business and some may come from the client or partner themselves (Figure 7.3).

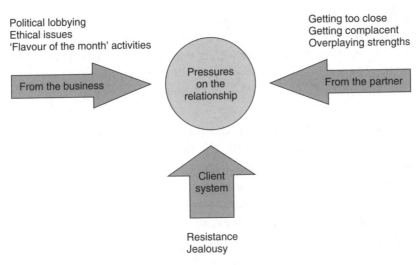

Political lobbying
Ethical issues
'Flavour of the month' activities

From the business

Pressures on the relationship

From the partner

Getting too close
Getting complacent
Overplaying strengths

Client system

Resistance
Jealousy

Figure 7.3   Pressures on the relationship

Pressures Stemming from the Business

Managing political pressures

Internal Business Partners are much more susceptible to political pressures due to their longer-term contract with the organisation, and they can sometimes be asked to bias a report or outcome to suit a particular audience. The more controversial the recommendations for change are the more likely it is that they will have added value for the organisation, but equally the more likely it is that there will also be political opposition to the suggestions.

This is no different to the pressure an external consultant might be put under and your credibility and business ethics are at stake in this situation. Unlike externals, however, there is a greater need to cover your own back as a Business Partner. Having put up an appropriate level of challenge to a politically led decision, a good approach would be to explicitly re-negotiate the terms of reference or to get agreement from the client so that you can make it clear to key members of the client system why a particular approach is being taken.

Dealing with ethical issues

However hard you plan for all eventualities and contract effectively with your client, it is likely that at some stage you will be put in a position which compromises your ethics to a degree. As a first step, with each project you need to know in advance what you are willing to do and approach the task with a clear view of what is and is not appropriate. However, you cannot plan for all eventualities. Cohen (1991) lists a number of ethical problems consultants face such as:

- Being asked to tailor a report to suit a particular audience and re-word your recommendations in some way to omit key information
- Being asked to deliver a particular solution to the problem that you know to be wrong or inappropriate
- Being asked to use information, as part of the data gathering, that was not gained in an open and honest way
- Being asked to set aside a contradictory finding to make the diagnosis easier.

A code of professional conduct, as discussed earlier, may help to address some of these issues. However, a clear sense of your own principles is often more important in helping you to make judgements when faced with ethical dilemmas. Lynch (1997 in Neumann) suggests that the two key tests for ethical dilemmas are:

- How transparent is the situation – that is, how much openness is there?
- How vulnerable are the stakeholders as a result of the proposed action?

If there is a lack of transparency, or the stakeholders may be vulnerable, then the consultant must weigh up their position and balance this against loyalty to their client. Lynch suggests it can often be useful to put the dilemmas into context by asking yourself questions such as:

- Have you defined the circumstance accurately?
- How did the situation occur?
- What is your role in it?
- Are you confident that your position is valid in the long term?
- Under what conditions would you allow exceptions to stand?
- What options do you have?
- What opportunities are there to discuss the situation with a third party?

- What are the consequences for each stakeholder as a result of your action or inaction?
- To whom and to what do you give your loyalty?
- Could your actions withstand cross-examination in a court by a barrister?
- Can you discuss the problem with the client before you make a decision?
- Would you feel comfortable explaining your behaviour to your family, friends and peers?
- Could you explain your actions to the media?

By answering these questions, the 'right' approach can often seem obvious. If this is not the case then, interestingly, the IMC has an ethical helpline which is aimed at providing confidential and non-judgemental feedback on ethical approaches.

Avoiding being drawn into 'flavour of the month'
It is easy to do what will please your client rather than what is right for the business, and Partners need to ensure they are continually managing internal customers as professionally as an external consultant would. Focus on activities that make a real impact on the business rather than getting led into 'flavour of the month' activities which will begin to devalue your impact. Business Partners need to use their judgement about what is right for the business and be prepared to challenge if they are asked to do work outside this scope.

In becoming a Business Partner, you are attempting to move internal relationships onto a more professional basis and provide a real improvement in business results. Establishing who are your prime customers and stakeholders and targeting them is a key part of this process. The initial contracting phase is critical in ensuring that your work is likely to add value.

Pressures Stemming from the Business Partner

Getting too close
Business Partners need to maintain independence from their client to avoid getting into a similar mindset where it is difficult to add value. Initially Partners can fall into the trap of working too much on the HR

147

agenda rather than respecting the client's agenda, but as the relationship grows there is also a need to maintain an emotional independence to prevent you from over-empathising with the client's position. Effective Partners will be prepared to speak their mind, air concerns and views and be open and honest about what they think and feel. Peter Block (2000) warns against identifying too closely with your clients. He states that we cannot view the client's triumphs and failures as a reflection of what we do or who we are – particularly if working in a process model. Gallwey (1997) distinguishes between 'Making something happen' and 'Letting something happen' (p. 36).

Getting complacent with good clients
When Business Partners achieve a strong relationship with their client, it becomes much easier to work with them. The meetings feel comfortable and relaxed and the themes emerging are likely to be familiar. Like any good partnership, there is a danger that the client and Partner begin to take each other for granted. Assumptions are made, rightly or wrongly, about what is required and the approach to be taken. Business Partners may even find themselves giving their established clients less of a priority and saying things like: 'I know you won't mind if . . .' or 'I'm sure you'll understand if I just . . .'.

It is essential that the Business Partner gives the same level of attention to established clients as to new ones. Trust and respect are easily broken in a relationship and not easily regained and often unintentional problems can begin to occur when the client and the Partner begin to make assumptions without conferring with each other.

Overplaying your key strengths
Effective relationships stem from an effective balance of your skills and strengths. If you have a particular strength it can be all too easy to over-use it and start to have a negative impact. For example, always acting with strong integrity or conviction can lead a client to view you as inflexible or arrogant. Even gaining too strong an empathy with a client can lead to a weakness stemming from over-identification with their issues at the exclusion of the bigger picture.

Sustaining a positive relationship with your client comes down to establishing an effective balance between a number of key characteristics:

Close	vs	Distant
Supportive	vs	Challenging
Integrity	vs	Inflexibility
Conviction	vs	Over-confidence or arrogance
Empathy	vs	Over-identification
Independence	vs	Aloofness

Pressures Stemming from the Client System

Viewing resistance as personal

No matter how good your rapport-building skills and credibility are, there is likely to come a time when the client puts up some resistance to progress. This can be a very frustrating time for the Partner, particularly as resistance is often due to an irrational behaviour stemming from the client's concerns.

One of the key skills of Business Partners is not to take the resistance personally and to help the client verbalise their position. It may be that the client is confused by the amount of information, or is feeling threatened by other people in the organisation. Some clients may just need time to see a particular perspective. The natural tendency when faced with resistance is to either back away or overly justify your position. However, it is at times like these that the relationship needs to become the focus rather than the project.

Often the resistance will not be received in an aggressive way, but will be indicated by passive behaviour such as limited feedback and lack of conviction through words like 'carry on, that's fine'. Sometimes the client will be constantly pressing for more information or evidence as a stalling mechanism, or will be more interested in the methodology than the solution. Only by drawing out what lies behind these states will the Partner be able to move forward. Peter Block in his book *Flawless Consulting* (2000) suggests using phrases such as: 'You seem to be willing to do anything I suggest. I can't tell what your real feelings are.' 'You are questioning a lot of what I do – you seem angry about something.'

The skills needed are excellent observation of the underlying feelings in the client and an ability to ask these more challenging questions about what is driving the behaviour.

Jealousy

If you are successful in your Business Partner role, build strong relationships with key players and are seen to have a positive impact on the business, it is possible that some of the client system or your peers could become jealous of your success. One Business Partner told us that dealing with jealousy was an unexpected challenge of their role, which has meant that they have to be extra-conscious of being open and approachable and not 'over-precious' about their role.

Summary

The ability to build strong and effective relationships is a key behaviour for Business Partners. Whilst some people naturally build rapport and empathy, it is a skill which can be developed and enhanced by being genuine with the client and trying to get a real understanding of their perspective. Empathetic relationships provide an essential foundation for starting to build credibility.

Credibility comes from both the individual and the more general perceptions of the Business Partnership Function. Individual credibility can be enhanced initially by going for quick wins, being responsive and generally being professional about the way messages are presented and how you use your expertise. To sustain individual credibility, you need to have conviction in what you say and do and be prepared to say no to work that does not add value to the business. Whilst it is important to work from the client's agenda rather than your own, you also need to ensure that you do not get emotionally drawn in and 'go native'.

Increasing the credibility of the Business Partnership Function comes from effective marketing. In addition to the marketing advice in Chapter 2, this involves gaining a sound understanding of the business; increasing visibility in key areas; using appropriate procedures and drawing on knowledge and expertise from inside or outside the company when it is needed.

Even when Business Partners have strong credibility, there will still be pressures and conflicts emerging. Political pressures from within organisations may lead to ethical dilemmas, and relationships may become strained if there is resistance to ideas or jealousy stemming from your success. Business Partners need to recognise these pressures and develop strategies to deal with them.

Checklist for the Quality of the Relationship

- You show a genuine interest in the client's issues
- You understand what makes your client tick on a personal and business level
- You are aware of the pressure faced by your client outside the project
- You notice and comment when the client behaves in a way which is inconsistent with their body language/meaning
- Your client responds positively when you summarise what has been talked about
- You do twice as much listening as talking when you are with your client
- You have a clear sense of your own preferences and principles
- You ensure that the client has clear expectations of the project deliverables
- You are often asked for advice by the client
- There is mutual trust at a professional level
- There is mutual trust at a personal level
- You enjoy spending time with your client
- The client comes to you to talk things over
- You are consistent in the message you give
- You have a clear understanding of the boundaries of confidentiality
- You collaborate extensively on the product or service
- You approach the client with new ideas or information they have not asked for
- You constantly deliver value related to the business
- The client does not check up on you
- You come across with conviction
- You resist taking sides and getting emotionally drawn into debates

- The client is understanding if you have pressures that prevent action
- The client believes you are competent to do the job
- The client values your integrity
- You spend time getting buy-in to the solution
- You are responsive to your client's needs
- You rarely take your client's needs or views for granted
- You have consistent and clear procedures to operate by
- You are prepared to challenge inappropriate recommendations or work
- You feel comfortable giving and receiving feedback to and from your client.

References

Block, P. (2000) *Flawless Consulting*, 2nd Edition, Jossey-Bass/Pfeiffer, San Francisco.

Cohen, W. A. (1991) *How to Make It Big as a Consultant*, Amacom, New York.

Gallwey, W. T. (1997) *The Inner Game of Tennis*, Random House, New York.

Maister, D., Green, C. and Galford, R. (2002) *The Trusted Advisor*, Simon and Schuster, London.

Neumann, J. E., Kellner, K. and Dawson-Shepherd, A. (1997) *Developing Organisational Consultancy*, Routledge, London.

Pfau, B. N. and Cundiff, B. B. (2002) '7 Steps Before Strategy', *Workforce*, Vol. 81, No. 12, November, pp. 40–44.

Sheth, J. and Sobel, A. (2000) *Clients for Life*, Fireside, New York.

8

Influencing and Leading Change

This chapter pays particular attention to the role of the Business Partner in influencing change and dealing with some of the reactions to change within the organisation. If you already have a seat at the strategic table and are considered one of a number of influential people who can support change within the business, then your job will be much easier. Some of you reading this book will be aspiring to the role of strategic Business Partner and so we hope you will find some useful pointers in this chapter on how to influence change in the organisation from a less strategic position too.

When we consider change in this chapter we are paying attention to interventions aimed at improving the business or performance of the business. As with previous chapters, we will draw on research and practice to illustrate both the challenges in implementing change and the methods and practices that have been successful.

What Kinds of Change are Business Partners Involved in?

Depending on the level at which the Business Partner sits, examples of change interventions might include the following:

- Implementing and facilitating mergers/acquisitions and partnerships
- Restructuring part or all of the company
- Introducing company-wide policies or systems
- Cultural change

- Reward and remuneration programmes
- Implementing people development strategies
- Recruitment and retention strategies
- Strategy on implementing legislative requirements – for example, around diversity
- Business process improvements.

All of these (and the list is not exhaustive) will have two key things in common. They should all have expected tangible business outcomes and they all have both task and people implications. If you are questioning the tangible business outcomes then that is likely to make your job of influencing change in the business much more difficult. A first step for the Business Partner is therefore clarifying the reasons for the change. One public-sector company we are involved with at the moment is making significant changes to their structure and processes as a result of the Modernising Government Agenda. This is resulting in some difficult questions about the purpose of the organisation: who the 'customer' really is and where the organisation should focus its energies for the future?

If Business Partners are truly working at a strategic level within their organisations, then an understanding of the nature of change at this level will be key to the success of the role. Questions for Business Partners around the implementation of change are likely to be:

- What are the business imperatives for this change?
- How can I get people alongside this change?
- What can I do if there is resistance?
- How can we achieve what is best for the business and manage the change in the timescale available?
- What methods are going to best fit the change that is required?
- Who needs to be involved? Why? How? And when?
- How will it affect me?

The last question is a fundamental one which is often ignored by people working inside the organisation. As Internal Consultants, we are often so busy dealing with the emotions of others that we forget to take stock of how changes are impacting on us – particularly at an emotional level. Many people within HR have found their own function being restructured over the last few years, and so being able to deal with the likely impact on you will be essential before supporting others to deal with some of the changes. We recently heard of a facilitator running a workshop who was so preoccupied with the changes going on in the organisation that they were coming back late to the start of sessions. Clearly this is not helpful for anyone.

Some options for dealing with your own emotions around the change include: having the conversations you need to before addressing others' concerns; putting it to one side emotionally until you can address it more fully or disclosing how you are feeling to your clients. The third option is likely to be more congruent but runs the risk of taking the focus off your client. We will look more closely at dealing with ambiguity as a part of the skills set for the Business Partner later in this chapter. We feel it is so important for HR to pay attention to their own process as well as supporting others in the organisation. Put aside some quality time with each other to see how people are; check out how you feel and are responding to the changes. Deal with your own 'stuff' so that you are better able to support others. Get outside help if you need to or if you notice yourself getting emotionally sucked into the challenges of change for others.

In this chapter we therefore consider the following:

- What is the nature of change?
- What are the boundaries of your role in influencing and leading change?
- Dealing with ambiguity
- What are the issues and implications of change for people in the organisation?
- What are some of the methods and models you might choose to use?
- Influencing strategies and styles
- Dealing with resistance
- Examples from companies of 'value-added' interventions.

What is the Nature of Change?

Emergent change and the principles of chaos and complexity (Stacey, 1996) are often quoted to help us understand that change is rarely a linear process and goes beyond predicting what the future might look like and planning a strategy to get there. These theories can be helpful for the Internal Consultant who may feel that there has to be a defined end point to their interventions. Business Partners and those in internal change agent roles can sometimes end up more as project managers if the boundaries are too tightly confined at the outset. Being clear about the purpose and values which underpin your role is probably more helpful than a tightly defined job description, so that you can flex your skills and experience to suit the needs of your clients.

Change in organisations today is rapid and complex. Perhaps one of the most common discussions we find ourselves having with individuals and groups in organisations is about the nature and speed of change. People seem to be overloaded with many change initiatives overlaying each other, causing an almost constant level of confusion and unsettlement.

In larger companies there are often a plethora of consultants working with the organisation to help on differing aspects of the business strategy. If these various interventions are not co-ordinated at a strategic level then confusion and chaos are likely to prevail. One important role for the Business Partner is to maintain sufficient clarity about the overall HR strategy for the business and how this links to the company strategy more widely.

We shall return briefly to systems theory and our example of the human body outlined in Part 1 – if one medical consultant is concerned with improving someone's blood pressure whilst another specialist advises on rheumatism without either talking about possible connections between the two, then the overall health of that individual is likely to be compromised.

'Chronic illness' is a term used when there is a long-standing and continuing health issue. There may be episodes of acute attacks (for example with asthma) but there is often an underlying chronic illness which also needs to be considered. Work therefore in a human system is often needed at a cellular level. In the same way, in organisational change, if we only treat the acute attacks – which might manifest as customer complaints about response times – the underlying and possible longer-term causes will not be addressed.

What are the Boundaries of Your Role in Influencing and Leading Change?

In Chapter 4 we considered perceptual positions as a way of positioning yourself with the client and other stakeholders. This can be a useful way to consider how to influence change in the organisation too. Starting with self: How are you experiencing the change? What will it mean to you? And, what are some of the beliefs and assumptions you might have about the change and how it should be managed?

Locus of control

The concept of locus of control is not a new one. Developed by Julian Rotter (in Pfeiffer, 1991), it is based on social learning theory which makes the link between expected outcomes and behaviour. Rotter's view was that if we believe that a certain outcome will happen we are more likely to act in a way which makes it so. This idea of self-fulfilling prophecy can work with either positive or negative results. So if I believe influencing change in this organisation is difficult and going to be wasted effort, then it is likely to be so. If, on the other hand, I believe that I have credibility and that people want and need to be engaged with the change process, then I am more likely to behave in a way that is congruent with those beliefs. This brings us back to the theme of our own underlying values and beliefs as an Internal Consultant and the importance of self-reflection for effective practice.

This is a useful model to consider, not just from a personal perspective for the Business Partner attempting to influence change, but also from the client's perspective. The more you can encourage people in the organisation to consider their own spheres of influence and control, the more likely they are to feel some sense of ownership for the change.

Difference between internal and external locus of control

Rotter (in Pfeiffer, 1991) used the term 'locus of control' to describe people who see control in terms of either being responsible for events (those who are internally focused) or being outside their control (externally focused). So that when something happens, which results in a positive outcome, someone with an external locus of control may see this as good luck. If something bad happens, it may be viewed as 'typical' or 'they always do that to me'. On the other hand someone who sees themselves as in part responsible for the outcome, whether positive or negative, is more likely to have an internal locus of control.

Business Partners may want to consider the following to help them prepare for influencing change in the organisation:

1. What, in relation to this change, is within my control right now? (This might include making decisions about who gets which post; how the change should be communicated and providing advice to senior managers on the next steps.)
2. What, in relation to this change, can I possibly influence? (This might include how the senior management team should deal with communicating the changes; what the company should decide to do when receiving hostile bids or how to change the policy on recruitment and retention.)
3. What, in the relation to this change, do I have no control over? (This might include the number of posts that have to be cut; amount of money available or who gets an influential senior management post.)

In our view it is always worth challenging further this third category. So even if it seems on a first take that you cannot influence the number of posts that have to be cut, you may be able to influence where those posts are taken from. The idea of considering 'locus of control' in this way is to really challenge your perception of what you have control over and to help minimise the amount of time and energy you might spend on areas that are beyond your spheres of influence.

Some questions you might usefully ask yourself at this stage:

- What has my previous experience been around organisational change?
- What do I know is helpful in times of change and what gets in the way?
- What do I think about the changes that I might need to implement and influence here?
- What are some of my beliefs and values about change?
- What is my role and what is the role of my internal clients?
- From a 'wise owl' perspective, how might the change best be implemented and managed?
- What are the benefits of this change to the organisation as a whole?
- What are the drivers behind it?

Dealing with Ambiguity

All of you reading this book, whether or not you have the title Business Partner, will have experienced change and the ambiguity that often surrounds it. When we find it difficult to find the one truth or one right course of action for making sense of change, then the level of ambiguity will be raised. However, the nature of humans is to make sense and meaning out of our experiences and so even if there is no one obvious way, we might find ourselves making connections and patterns to ease the sense of uncertainty that is around. So often we find ourselves talking to managers, particularly in the middle levels of an organisation, who feel there must be an answer somewhere on the direction of the company and what the future holds in store. However, it is also our experience that 'the future' is becoming increasingly difficult for senior managers to predict. When no-one apparently has the answers, the Business Partner can find themselves in the uncomfortable position of carrying much of the ambiguity that surrounds the change for others in the organisation as well as themselves.

Managing or, perhaps more appropriately, living with ambiguity, involves being able to let go of what is familiar and certain. Here are some ways of stretching your comfort zones around dealing with ambiguity:

- Delegate a pet project (if you have the resources to do this) and try letting go of the control over something you enjoy.
- Rather than coming up with expert solutions to some of your client's issues, try saying 'I don't know' once in a while or 'what do you think?' and resist giving the answer for longer than you currently do.
- Use lateral thinking approaches, such as board storming or Thinking Hats (De Bono, 1996) to open up the possible ways of approaching issues and problems.
- Put off making a decision if you tend to always make these quickly, just to see what happens.
- Consider doing nothing as an intervention option and see what impact this has.
- Use re-framing as a way of looking at things from a different perspective; for example, 'what if we imagined everyone in the organisation welcomed this change?'

Ambiguity – when it exists in one area of our life it is one thing. When we find there is too much ambiguity around in both our work and home lives, then this can cause stress and anxiety overload. It is worth thinking about your own personal levels of comfort around ambiguity and doing what you can and need to in stabilising those areas that you are able to. For example, if you are dealing with a good deal of complex and challenging change at work, that might not be the best time to move house. Having said this, we accept that it is not always possible to create stability in this way and so coping strategies might more helpfully be adopted. Chapter 6 mentions some tips on supporting self in the challenging role of Business Partner.

What are the Issues and Implications for Others in Times of Change?

Continuing with perceptual positions, it would be useful early on in the change process to consider how different stakeholders will be experiencing the change and what their likely reactions to this might be. For the most part, even when people know the changes are needed from an organisational perspective, there is likely to be a focus on how the changes will affect them as individuals – the 'what's in it for me?' factor.

Reactions to change – the human element

When major change takes place within an organisation, the reactions of individuals and groups cannot always be easily determined. Many of our readers will be familiar with the idea of the transition curve, much used when considering the emotional stages of change that individuals might experience from shock/denial, depression and eventual acceptance and integration. Because of the rate of change in organisations, it is not always easy to read reactions. For example, one individual or group might be stuck in denial or blame (of themselves or others), whereas another might be through to acceptance. Where change has been orchestrated by the senior managers, it is common to find acceptance at that level while others in the organisation might be further back on the curve. If senior managers feel they have to shield employees from sharing in the ambiguity and uncertainty that often goes alongside change, this can frustrate even further.

The Business Partner may find in their close alignment with the senior managers in the organisation that they too have moved more quickly through to acceptance and integration. There is a danger here that you may lose sight of how the changes are being received at a grass-roots level. A careful balance needs to be maintained between staying closely aligned to the main needs of your clients (probably the more senior managers in the organisation) and being attuned to the needs of other stakeholders.

Agyris and Schon (1978) developed the notion of the learning organisation and how organisations adapt to change internally and externally through single and double loop learning. Single loop learning is fixed and non-adaptive. In organisations it tends towards procedures and adapting procedures to maintain stability. Managers here may make adjustments and change but because underlying principles are not challenged, it is more likely that the status quo will prevail. Trial and error is an example of single loop learning. In this type of learning, the focus is on using feedback to decide what to do better next time. Generative or double loop learning is where the individual or organisation allows their mental models to be influenced and perhaps changed by the feedback. This is about questioning assumptions and learning to learn – seeing situations in differing ways. Double loop learning in times of change means seeking information on which to make choices and involving others through discussion. The learning here is through challenging long-standing beliefs and inviting approaches which might be uncomfortable. This approach is more likely to find underlying causes and needs for change for individuals and the organisation overall.

Change interventions which generate learning

The title 'large-scale interventions for change' is often given to a range of activities or interventions in organisations aimed at facilitating rapid change. Examples used here include Open Space Technology, Real Time Strategic Change, Future Search and Appreciative Inquiry. One of the key principles is that of engaging as many people in the 'system' as in the change itself. So that rather than a select group of people deciding what the changes should be and how they should be progressed, a critical mass of employees would have a say in both the what and the how. These interventions are then based around a conference usually lasting from one to three or four days.

People are invited to participate in the process of change so that they:

- Understand the need for change
- Participate in making sense of the current reality and decisions about what needs to change
- Generate ideas about how to change existing processes
- Engage with the implementation phase(s) and make things happen in reality.

The beauty of these large-scale interventions is that they challenge some of the traditional assumptions about change – that is, it has to be slow and painful. Assumptions which underpin a range of interventions in this category include:

- Change happens most successfully when people have a say in the changes which will affect them
- The people who are closest to the issues often have critical information which is vital to share for the overall benefit of the organisation
- By engaging a critical mass of people at the same time, the information and change strategy will be enriched
- Synergy can lead to innovation and creative change strategies
- Diversity of people and ideas is more likely to lead to good solutions
- Change can happen quickly.

There are some important underlying principles and values which underpin large-scale change interventions when applied purely (adapted from Bunker and Alban, 1997):

- Engagement
- Selecting the right issue
- Selecting the right people
- Structuring the intervention
- Paying attention to the process.

Engagement
Underpinning all the interventions that normally come into the category 'large-scale intervention' is one of valuing engagement. It is key that if a critical mass of people within the organisational system are to be invited

to take part in the change strategy and process, then a real belief in the value of engagement needs to be present. There are many examples of people being invited to take part in discussions around the future of the organisation only to find that their views are either ignored or given a token airing.

For engagement to really work and become meaningful for individuals and groups there needs to be a commitment to hearing and taking on board the views of people at the conference and a willingness to learn from what is being said. This means an attitude of openness and curiosity on behalf of everyone present – particularly important for the Business Partner, if this is an intervention which you consider using.

Selecting the right issue

The main consideration here is that the issue should be systemic. In other words, it needs to be something which affects the system overall. It should also be important enough for people to want to air their views on it. For example, the values of the organisation; reward and recognition strategies; improving customer service; improving quality of products, etc. would be examples of what might be systemic issues. The subject needs to be sufficiently focused so that it is clear what the theme for the conference will be. The planning group (mentioned below) will normally help to shape how the issue is presented to make that clearer for the conversations. It needs to be meaningful for all those attending including any external stakeholders who are invited to take part. Having a positive and future-focused spin on the issue will help to steer clear of a problem-solving approach and free up lateral thinking. Examples might include:

■ Creating excellent customer service
■ Rewarding people to reflect their value and contribution
■ Creating a community of best practice
■ Reflecting positively on the communities we serve
■ Getting the right products in place at the right time
■ Developing leading edge practice in research
■ Creating a 'fit for purpose' structure which meets business needs.

Selecting the right people

A planning group will normally be set up of people who represent a microcosm of the organisation and its stakeholders. One of the main tasks for this planning group is to decide who should be at the event. The focus for deciding is the primary question that needs to be addressed as outlined in the above section. Stakeholder mapping as described in Chapter 4 can be used to determine who needs to be present. Bunker and Alban (1997) give a nice example of a school system holding a meeting about an education issue and inviting a taxpayer organisation. It might be worth thinking about who would be your organisational critics and the potential value of inviting them along as outside stakeholders. The conference will also provide a good opportunity for the senior managers in the organisation to have a visible presence, although they will need to be seen to be encouraging engagement by everyone in the organisation, rather than imposing their own view of change.

Structuring the intervention

A key part of these interventions is to enable people at all levels in the organisation and sometimes outside stakeholders to have a voice. Change can feel incredibly disempowering if people do not feel like they have had an opportunity to participate in the process. The design and structure of the intervention therefore needs to create opportunities for people to talk and listen to each other. One important reason why these conferences are usually over more than one day is the opportunity for reflection time. Real Time Strategic Change, for example (Dannemiller and Jacobs in Bunker and Alban, 1997), is based around the Beckhard and Harris model of change (Beckhard and Harris, 1987):

$$C = D \times V \times F > R$$

The model states that change will happen when there is sufficient dissatisfaction (D) with the present status quo; when there is a clear vision of the future (V) and some tangible first steps (F). All three elements have to be greater than any resistance to the change or perceived cost. If any element is not present then the change process can get stuck.

In an intervention which helps people move through these stages, dissatisfaction is sometimes heightened during the first day of the conference, by holding up the proverbial mirror, sometimes by speeches from external stakeholders or clients so that there is impetus to move from the present unsatisfactory position. Therefore, the first night of a conference structured with this in mind allows people to face the reality of the current status, before moving on to the vision for the future.

The right level of structure for these events is important. If it is too structured people become anxious and if it is not structured enough people can become anxious, so boundary management is important. Generally speaking the structure needs to be designed around the process rather than the content of the discussions.

Organisations that have attempted to speed up the process and deal with all these aspects within a day may have found that although energy is present and people are full of good intentions, there has been insufficient time and attention paid to really bottoming out all of the issues. Sustained change is less likely in these scenarios.

Paying attention to the process
As these events usually involve large numbers (anywhere from 35 to over a 1000), the structure and process issues are crucially important. Tables are normally set up carousel style with groups of approximately six people sitting at each in a max-mix style (people from different stakeholder groups at each table). The timing and logistics for these large-scale events is crucial. People need to move through the process smoothly, often looking back in some way at the history of either the issue or the organisation; looking forward to the vision for the future and focusing on actions to get there. Creating the right dynamic for people to discuss things in an open environment and feel committed to taking things forward takes light-handed but skilled facilitation and many Internal Consultants who want to try these methods work with externals skilled in using the frameworks and in facilitating the process.

As examples of the methods you may use to take people through the various stages: storytelling and an environmental scan could be used to bring out the past; board storming in groups for considering the present and future around some questions – What should we stop doing? What should we continue doing? And what should we create? – to look at how you want to get to where you want to be. Another method commonly used is that of a 'marketplace' with stalls for various stakeholder groups or topics. In Open Space Technology, people decide on which topic they want to discuss within a broad conference theme. The 'law of 2 feet' gives them permission to stay or leave the discussion when they decide.

With all these methods, the responsibility and ownership for the outcomes remains firmly with the people attending the conference. It is crucial that sufficient time is built in for action planning and follow-up if the change is to be followed through.

Who uses large-scale interventions?

From Roffey Park's Management Agenda (2003) with 235 respondents, we find that 18 per cent of those responding reported that they used large-scale interventions to involve people in strategy-making processes.

The key strategy developers within organisations appear to be top managers only (44%) and a combination of top managers and middle managers (46%). Additionally designated teams (32%) and people at all levels (25%) are also referred to. Respondents were also asked how people are involved in the strategy-making processes. The majority pointed to direct involvement in planning processes (71%) through idea sharing (48%) and through surveys (29%). Large-scale interventions (18%) were referred to but to a lesser extent.

We also sent a web survey to 647 Roffey Park contacts by e-mail. Forty-three people completed the survey and several others responded by e-mail. Respondents were mostly from the private services sector (47.5%) but other sectors were also represented (15% from production and manufacturing, 27.5% public sector, 10% charity/not for profit). They came from organisations of all sizes.

Of the 43 respondents, just over half (53.5%) reported that their organisation had undergone a large-scale intervention to support change. Six (14%) had used Open Space Technology, seven (16.3%) had used Real Time Strategic Change, five (11.6%) had used Appreciative Inquiry and six (14%) had used Future Search. Other methods were reported including Action Labs, motivational communication events, organisational transformation framework and employee engagement surveys.

Organisations who had engaged in large-scale interventions most commonly used external facilitators (60.9%). Almost half used HR to facilitate and the same proportion used senior managers. Other facilitators included OD specialists.

Other Aspects of Change

The model given in Figure 8.1 highlights aspects of change that might need to be considered if the change is to be managed effectively. The highlighted areas show the likely impact if any of these elements are missing. So, where there is a lack of vision, but all the other aspects of the equation are in place, you may find there is a high level of confusion in the organisation, or part of the organisation affected by the change.

As we can see, any of the missing elements can trigger either an emotional response or a lack of effective transition to the desired future. Even if the vision to the desired future is not entirely clear, people will need to have a sense of where they are headed to feel that their day-to-day efforts are not entirely in vain.

You might find it useful to reflect on the following in relation to changes you are trying to influence in your organisation:

- How clear is the vision or desired future goal for this change?
- What skills do people need to effect the changes? Who needs which skills? And how can they best be developed?

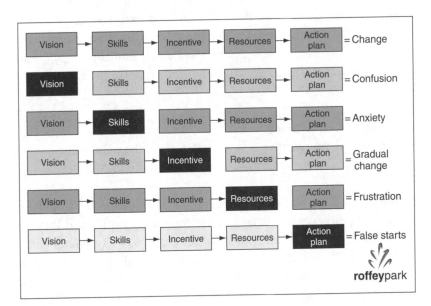

Figure 8.1 Managing the change process

- What incentives are already in place or could be put in place? These do not necessarily need to be financial, but what might be the benefit to individuals and groups of the changes that are needed?
- What resources are needed? This might include equipment, access to people, access to information, etc. and how can you make sure people have access to the resources that they will need?
- What steps are needed to make the change happen? If there is no formal project plan for this piece of work, calculating the milestones will still be helpful.

When considering methods for implementing change it will be important to focus on the outcome you are seeking to achieve. Success, in our view, is more likely if an iterative approach is taken. This means more than one intervention is aimed at achieving the end result with opportunities to reflect on the impact of the interventions at each stage. Our case studies at the end of this chapter bear this out.

Influencing Skills and Strategies

The Business Partner will need to draw on a range of influencing strategies, skills and styles to be effective at implementing change at all levels in the organisation. We looked at political skills in our earlier chapter, and influencing and political skills are in many ways interlinked. Both skills sets can be used either ethically or not, and with an understanding of the culture of the organisation and dynamics or not.

Core skills of influencing

In our view, if you want to be more influential, there are some underpinning aspects of these skills that might be helpful to consider:

- We all have the ability to influence – it is happening all the time. Just try smiling at someone and see what happens. Even if they do not smile back you will probably get a reaction. By doing something either unconsciously or consciously we will have an impact on someone else. For example, not turning up at a meeting.
- Much influencing behaviour is outside the conscious awareness of the people involved.

- We cannot change other people's behaviour, we can only change/adapt our own behaviour and by doing that it may cause the other to change.
- Most influencing is concerned more with the process than with the content.

If you have ever been influenced to buy something you were not particularly interested in, when you return home you will understand this last point.

We have referred to some of the skills elsewhere in the book, but by way of summary we would see these as being:

- **Self-awareness** – understanding how you typically react to difficult situations and being able to increase your range of choices in how you react and behave.
- **Self-confidence** – based on self-acceptance. The ability to feel confident in your own internal and external resources in the face of resistance.
- **Observation skills** – the ability to pick up on content and process messages (i.e. the non-verbal behaviour).
- **Interpretation** – making sense of what is going on at the moment, based on both self-awareness and wider awareness.
- **Listening** – actively and attentively to what others are really saying.
- **Questioning** – knowing when to ask open and closed questions, and asking them at the appropriate level; for example, facts or feelings.
- **Having an outcome focus** – being clear about what you want from the interaction.
- **Ability to see things from different perspectives**.
- **Flexible communication skills** – the ability to put your message across in a variety of ways to suit the style of the other person/group.
- **Timing** – the ability to judge when it is appropriate to have a conversation with someone or when to take action.

Push and pull strategies for influencing

We are going to cover here push and pull strategies for influencing which can be used in a one-to-one, group or organisational context. Both push and pull strategies are really about how we use our energy – energy used to push someone or something in a particular direction or to draw them towards our way of thinking.

Force-field analysis as a diagnostic tool
We touched on force-field analysis in Chapter 4 as a way of considering the driving and resisting forces for the HR move into strategic Business Partnership. Here we re-visit the model in more detail and link it to interventions for influencing change.

Push and pull strategies as a way of influencing change
As a Business Partner you can increase your range of options for influencing a change by considering push and pull strategies. For example, in the case of a recent restructure where jobs are being re-advertised and redundancies may follow.

Examples of push strategies might include
Top-down communication which sets out clearly what is happening and why, statements about what is not negotiable, decisions made already and telling people what the jobs will be and when they will be invited to apply.

Advantages of this approach are that it tends to be quicker; people know where they stand and in times of uncertainty a sense of direction from the top can be reassuring.

Disadvantages – as you can imagine, people can feel uninvolved and undervalued, as if their views do not count. The organisation might miss out on some good ideas about the way forward. People affected by the change may be the very people who have the best ideas for improving the way things are.

Examples of pull strategies might include
Providing opportunities for discussions, Q&A sessions; getting people involved in what the re-structure would look like and writing the job descriptions.

Advantages of this approach are that people are more likely to be committed to the outcome if they have been involved from the outset. Any ambiguity and fear around the change is shared, rather than protecting people unnecessarily. People get the full picture earlier and can make their own choices about what to do, which may include looking for other jobs.

Disadvantages – Time is the biggest one. It takes longer to be consultative. People's expectations might be raised and you need to be sure that the consultation is a genuine one, otherwise there could be many disgruntled employees who feel that they have been asked for views which are not going to be taken on board.

For long-term change strategies, a combination of both will be necessary. Some examples of combined strategies to deal with the re-structuring example above are shown below:

- Communicating clearly what is negotiable and what is not – message from the top
- Regular bulletins and updates via a variety of methods, for example, e-mail, newsletters, intranet
- Providing forums for discussion and answering questions
- Workshops on change management
- Training for those applying for new/existing jobs
- Project groups across the organisation to look specifically at aspects of the work that need to change
- Outplacement counselling where necessary.

Both can be very effective and it is important to have enough flexibility of style to be able to draw on the appropriate skills at the right time.

In our view, push and pull behaviours are still responsive to the situation and the individuals; therefore they are all assertive in nature, rather than tipping into aggressive or passive behaviour which tends to be reactive rather than responsive.

For short-term outcomes, for example to consider influencing someone in a discussion on a one-to-one basis or at a meeting, you might want to consider which set of behaviours would be more influential – push or pull.

Push behaviour
Push behaviour includes being directive (i.e. telling rather than asking); giving information; using facts and logic; enforcing the rules; and applying sanctions and pressures.

Pull behaviour
Pull behaviour includes drawing others out; offering incentives and rewards; finding the common threads between differing views; and inspiring others towards a shared goal.

It is worth considering if you tend to use the full range of influencing skills or whether you tend to rely on either push or pull to achieve your desired outcome. Training in influencing skills can help to develop a wider range of skills and strategies.

Business Partners can also coach managers to help them develop a greater range of influencing skills. In this way, managers are more likely to be able to facilitate change within the organisation effectively.

Dealing with Resistance to Change

Sometimes when attempting to influence organisational change, even if you have used a wide range of strategies and involved people in the organisation, you will be met by resistance and conflict. We believe you are more likely to experience resistance if you expect it, but you may also get it if you do not.

Resistance to change can be observed in a number of ways:

- Overt conflict and arguments between either individuals or teams
- Withdrawal or apathy about the issue, detachment and disengagement
- Increased political behaviour (see Chapter 6)
- Drop in performance or productivity
- Lack of teamwork, more individualistic behaviour
- Increased grapevine and gossip.

Conflict is often perceived to be negative and as an obstruction to progress. However, conflict can also be a positive energy and a catalyst for movement. Two roles for the Business Partner in helping support others through the change process are that of mediator and coach. While it would be unrealistic to expect all Business Partners to be trained and experienced in both these skills to the level of full-time mediators and coaches, having an understanding of the skills and being able to apply a sufficient level will prove very useful, particularly in managing change.

A recent example which comes to mind includes again a restructure within an organisation where individuals in previously secure employment were required to be interviewed for their present jobs, sometimes in competition with close colleagues. There was a great deal of unrest and anger at the 'management' in the organisation for seemingly putting them in this difficult position. While the changes were accepted on an intellectual level as being necessary for the business, there was a good deal of dissatisfaction around how the process had been managed. The Business Partner was called in to help facilitate the change process.

Clearly coaching the senior managers to handle this change would be a useful part of the change strategy. Preferably the Business Partner would be asked to help on this before decisions had been made and action taken. However, in this situation the Business Partner was called in after the event – to help mop up the pieces. Where the closest client is the senior manager, mediation in the true sense can be difficult. One of the important principles behind mediation is that of neutrality. If the various parties involved in the conflict do not see you as neutral then mediation will be difficult and you may need to call for outside help. The key skills in both coaching and mediation include active listening, asking open and probing questions, reflecting back at a content and process level, offering insights on how you see the situation and the behaviours, helping people to re-frame the situation, gaining clarity about what people want and need to move forward, and agreeing actions.

Coaching from the Business Partner can happen on both an informal and a formal level. One of the more successful interventions towards change is that of informal coaching of senior managers. Coaching also happens at the early stage of 'gaining entry' referred to in Chapter 4 and throughout developing the consultant–client relationship. Knowing when to use a directive or non-directive style in coaching is important. Non-directive coaching, where you allow the manager to make their own choices for how to move forward, is more likely to help in strategies aimed at long-term change.

Styles of intervention from acceptant to prescriptive can usefully be considered when coaching your internal clients (Cockman et al., 1992)

Acceptant style
This includes listening in a neutral, non-judgemental way to help relax clients and allow them to confront any blocks at an emotional level in moving forward. It is likened to the early stages of counselling. Here positive regard and empathy will help the client to talk freely.

When is it appropriate?
This can be particularly useful at the early stages of a consultant–client relationship or when the client is experiencing pain around something

that is impacting them on a personal or organisational level. It can also be a useful style to adopt with teams or groups who are experiencing problems with change and expressing anger or anxiety.

Catalytic style

The skills here include asking questions and gathering data with the purpose of helping the client to generate ideas to solve issues themselves. Questions usefully asked here start with: who, what, why, how, where, when and how. The CONSULT framework in Chapter 4 gives some examples of this approach.

When is it appropriate?

It is appropriate when the client or group is in a resourceful state and needs help in generating thinking more clearly about the issues. The ways of generating information can include a number of differing methodologies, not just face-to-face questioning. It is a helpful part of the data gathering and diagnostic stage for both the consultant and the client.

Confrontational style

This style is epitomised by 'holding up the mirror' so that the client can gain insight into what is really going on. The consultant calls attention to differences between values and behaviours, or the espoused theories and those in use. The skills here would include feedback and presenting information in a way which confronts the ongoing issues about what you notice.

When is it appropriate?

It is appropriate when you have built up sufficient trust with the client or when there is no other option. In other words, if you think your client will not move on without a level of confrontation on the issues then this may be the best way forward. When the interests of other clients or stakeholders in the change need to be reflected back, then your client needs to be made fully aware of the big picture.

Prescriptive style

This links most closely to the Expert or doctor–patient model in our earlier chapter. It involves giving advice and expertise and providing data on the issue presented to you by the client.

When is it appropriate?

Sometimes this is a good way to build trust with your clients, particularly those who are looking for an expert view. It is worth being wary here of staying in the role too long in case the client becomes dependant on you providing this service, when they may have the capacity to move things forward themselves.

By developing and extending your style and skills in coaching you will be adding to your already wide skills set and heightening your ability to influence change in the organisation.

Value-added Interventions

We asked a number of people in the role of Business Partner (although not necessarily with that title) for examples of what they felt were 'value-added interventions' for HR working more strategically within their organisation. What follows are summaries of some of these discussions, which help to give a better understanding of how Business Partners manage change in practice.

Chevron Texaco Upstream Europe

Howard Kewney, HR Manager

Influencing leadership was discussed as an important area for the Business Partners to impact.

The role of the supervisor in performance management, employee development and pay determination is critical in an organisation that rewards for performance, yet the linkage between performance measurement and pay is little understood by the workforce.

The processes within the organisation are well-defined and well-established, yet the understanding among employees is very limited. There is a lack of appreciation of the role that the supervisor plays in determining an individual's pay, and overall a mistrust of the system.

This year the HR function has taken the initiative to design and roll out a series of workshops to all employees to help them understand the process and remove any mystery that may previously have existed.

These workshops were run by the department/team in groups of around 15–20 with the supervisor present. Prior to the employee workshops, supervisor workshops were held to ensure that supervisors understood and supported the process, and were able to assist with questions from their group, and re-enforce the messages about the process. This gave them the opportunity to role model leadership behaviours and to take on the responsibility of ownership rather than allowing it to be seen purely as an HR activity.

Key learnings and outcomes can be summarised as follows:

■ The box has been opened, leading to a greater understanding among employees
■ The importance of clear objectives and constructive discussion on achievements between employee and supervisor and how this impacts pay has become clearer
■ For employees, the recognition that their supervisor plays a critical role in representing them in the employee-ranking sessions
■ For supervisors, the increased understanding that their employees place a greater responsibility on them to ensure that they get it right
■ An enlightened workforce will constructively challenge the processes with more knowledge of the system and ensure that management continues to improve them.

The key messages from this for Howard are that influencing can come in many forms and shades. This intervention was not primarily intended to change management attitudes or behaviours, but the process will encourage employees to influence upwards which in turn will influence supervisor's behaviour.

Other aspects of influencing change include:

■ Determining how much time you are spending on operational issues against the more strategic work
■ Keeping the ratio of time spent influencing management high, by asking them how things are going and keeping a regular connection with them
■ Supporting managers to think about the business in the long term – for example, what the business demands will be in 2010.

In Howard's view all of these require a high level of interpersonal skill with coaching being a key part of the role.

Home Office, Human Resources Directorate

Tracy McGee, HR Business Partner
Tracy was involved in a TUPE-like transfer (TUPE – Transfer of Undertakings [Protection of Employment] Regulation 1981) of approximately 250 staff from the Department for Education and Skills (DfES) to the Home Office. The staff in the Work Permits UK area were required to transfer under the machinery of Government legislation, and Tracy's role as the Senior HR Advisor at the time was to ensure their smooth transition.

Challenges included providing the same or improved terms and conditions for the transferred staff whose grades ranged from Director to the more junior levels in the organisation.

The perceived difference in values and culture of the two organisations was a potential barrier to a smooth transition. There was a lack of clarity about the ability to preserve terms and conditions for the new staff and DfES staff were concerned about some issues surrounding their transfer to the Home Office. Building trust and understanding were therefore key.

The change strategy for helping smooth the transition included:

- Getting a seat on the Senior Management Team of Work Permits UK
- Working out the terms and conditions so that staff would face no detriment in joining the Home Office
- Working alongside the DfES and maintaining good relationships with the HR team there
- Ensuring that access to benefits such as health and welfare met the staff needs
- Reconciling recruitment practices between the two organisations
- Spending time with the new staff in Sheffield
- Making sure managers had access to seminars on any new procedures
- Arranging for 'drop in' surgeries for managers and junior staff
- Being available on a week-by-week basis
- Selling the benefits – for example, improved promotion opportunities
- Ensuring the HR team were kept up to date on events.

A key point in the transition seemed to be the fiscal relocation of one of the Senior Directors to Sheffield where the DfES staff were based. This signalled a positive move towards integration.

The Trade Union Side were also instrumental (within both the Home Office and the DfES) in helping to get the changes pushed through.

Key learning and outcomes can be summarised as follows:

- Keeping a visible presence and maintaining communication channels
- Building up relationships and trust
- Delivering on what you say you can
- Providing dedicated teams on specific queries – for example pay
- Never assume you know the issues
- Getting your face known
- Working in partnership, particularly around recruitment
- DfES staff are now more integrated within the Immigration and Nationality Directorate and also with regions outside Sheffield.

Severn Trent Water

Jane Miller, Learning and Development Manager
Developing and delivering a pay system which linked performance to salary was a huge scale change where Jane felt Business Partners had to influence behavioural change in the organisation.

The new pay system meant Line Managers were in a position to influence people's individual pay rewards and so the strategy for introducing the change needed careful consideration.

The range of interventions which were part of this change strategy included:

- Joint implementation teams working at both strategic and operational levels across HR and management
- Communication and updates – particularly monthly team briefings including reminders of the impending new process, so that this could be cascaded down the line
- Articles in company magazines, to give the big picture view of what was happening
- Newsletters were issued every couple of months which were e-mailed to managers (approx. 160) with suggestions to print these out and put them on notice boards

- Staff were invited to a workshop to help them understand how pay would link to performance in the future
- Training delivered by both HR and Line Managers
- Frequently asked questions on the intranet which could be accessed by HR and managers.

As a minimum people were invited to a workshop, they were all issued a handbook on pay, performance and rewards. The same booklet was issued for managers and staff, modelling an intention of transparency and openness.

Extra training programmes in performance management were planned throughout the implementation period to ensure there was sufficient opportunity for those who needed to improve their skills to be able to do so.

Managers attended workshops in the early part of the appraisal year so that they understood the implications of the revised system. Subsequent briefings meant they knew the importance of measuring performance success and outcomes. At the end of the year they also had briefing sessions so that they were clear on how to give performance ratings to their staff. Later in the year, a follow-up half-day workshop supported the managers in communicating the subsequent pay awards to their staff. Letters would be personally delivered to individuals by their Line Managers and so needed careful handling.

The managers, according to Jane, mostly wanted to get involved in the process so that they had some control over pay and rewards. They wanted more flexibility in the pay awards and to have a say in pay differentials. Having more say in pay differentials went hand in hand with the sometimes difficult messages that managers would also have to give to certain staff.

Key learning and outcomes can be summarised as follows:

- Keeping the communication going alongside actions
- Training workshops were tailored to specific work groups
- Departments took the opportunity to integrate the introduction of this new system with other changes they wanted to make – this ensured consistency and a more holistic approach
- Securing and maintaining the ownership of the process by Line Managers is critical

- The HR team needed to keep in touch regularly to share thoughts on how and what to communicate
- Not feeling like you have to have all the answers
- Keeping open to an evolving and iterative process
- All pay changes were made on time
- From an audit of 500 staff (48% returned the questionnaire) 92 per cent of respondents understand what their manager expects of them
- 93 per cent felt their appraiser's expectations of them were fair
- 91 per cent felt they can have an open and honest discussion with their appraiser about their performance and behaviour
- 93 per cent agree that their appraiser listens to their views about their job and performance.

Summary

The ability to influence and lead change is perhaps the key area that sets apart the truly strategic Business Partner from the more operational HR role. As someone working inside the organisation, there will be challenges that present themselves over and above the challenges that are present for external consultants. By understanding the nature of change and how change impacts on people at all levels of the organisation, you are more likely to approach your projects with an appropriate balance of attention to task and process issues. Supporting managers, particularly at the senior levels of the organisation, will be an important and useful way of influencing how change is dealt with for the longer term. If the senior managers in the organisation are equipped to lead change well, the implementation process is likely to be eased. The ability to coach in both formal and informal situations and influence the way the changes are handled requires high levels of skill and understanding. Supporting yourself through the change and managing the personal impact on you is also important so that you are more able to support others through this process. Influencing, coaching and mediation skills may all come into play in your role in supporting strategic change.

In this part we have covered some skills which we consider key to the role of successful Business Partnership – in particular, contracting, self-awareness and critical reflection; building and maintaining effective relationships; and influencing and leading change. We appreciate that there could be a number of other chapters including skills such as project management, strategic thinking and strategy implementation. However, we have decided to focus on those areas which we think are at the core of the role and less structured in their approach.

Checklist

- Are you clear on how the various initiatives and external consultant activities tie in with the strategic business plan?
- Have you got a support strategy for helping you deal with your own reactions to the changes going on in the organisation?
- Have you established those areas that you either have direct control over or can influence?
- Have you let go of the areas that you cannot influence?
- Are you creating some stability in your life to help support the areas that are more ambiguous and uncertain?
- Are you checking out how people in the organisation are responding to change?
- Have you considered engaging more people in the change process? – either by using large-scale interventions or by applying the principles?
- Do people at all levels in the organisation feel like they have a 'voice' to explore the change strategy and their views on it? How do you know?
- Is there a clear vision to support the changes?
- Are you increasing your range of influencing skills and strategies to good effect?
- Are you identifying and dealing with any resistance to change?
- Are you using your skills to coach managers, either formally or informally, to help them deal with the change process in the most appropriate way?
- Are you using a range of interventions to help implement the changes that are needed in the organisation?

References

Agyris, C. and Schon, D. (1978) *Organisational Learning: A Theory of Action Perspectives*, Addison-Wesley, Reading, Mass.

Beckhard, R. and Harris, R. (1987) *Organisational Transformations: Managing Complex Change*, Addison-Wesley, Reading, Mass.

Bunker, B. and Alban, B. T. (1997) *Large Group Interventions: Engaging the Whole System for Rapid Change*, Jossey-Bass, San Francisco.

Cockman, P., Evans, B. and Reynolds, P. (1992) *Client-centred Consulting: A Practical Guide for Internal Advisers and Trainers*, McGraw-Hill, Maidenhead.

De Bono, E. (1996) *Serious Creativity: Using the Power of Lateral Thinking to Create New Ideas*, HarperCollins Business, London.

Pfeiffer & Company (1991) *Theories and Models in Applied Behavioural Science Volume 4: Organisational*, Pfeiffer & Company, San Diego, CA.

Stacey, R. D. (1996) *Complexity and Creativity in Organisations*, Berrett-Koehler Publishers Inc., San Francisco.

Part 3

Assessing Your Progress

This part focuses on one of the key sets of behaviours required of any Business Partner, to ensure that they are focusing on the key requirements for the business as a whole rather than just delivering to the client's needs. In doing this, they also need to ensure that they are performing as effectively as possible in any work they undertake.

Chapter 9 examines the process of reviewing performance and eliciting feedback from the client system. One aspect of the feedback process is aimed at Business Partners assessing their own performance from the perspective of themselves, the client and other people in the client system. The other aspect is to review the effectiveness of the process used for the work, as distinct from the measurement of the value added by a particular project. The chapter also examines a topic which many Internal Consultants find difficult, which is to draw a close to projects they are working on and move on from a piece of work without impacting relationships amongst those remaining. This process begins by recognising the need for closure on a particular project and positioning the client so that you can both move on.

Chapter 10 examines the difficult topic of measuring the impact of the Business Partner role to gain some evidence to demonstrate the added value of the role and measure progress in terms of the outputs. Evaluation is a difficult topic and one which few companies have got to grips with, so the chapter starts by examining what gets in the way of evaluation and setting out some good practice guidelines to help establish a focus on evaluation. The chapter then moves on to outline some of the models of evaluation stemming from traditional HR and OD that might apply to Business Partnerships and ends by focusing on more recent Business Partner models.

The behaviours from our model in Part 1 are concerned with maintaining a business focus. This includes prioritising effectively, utilising feedback and demonstrating effectiveness by setting appropriate measures and ensuring buy-in to the evaluation process. In particular it is critical that Business Partners obtain and utilise business data and seek to improve their service and gain insights from the feedback they receive.

9

Reviewing Performance

Reviewing performance and eliciting feedback from the client system can take place at any time throughout a project and continual feedback should be encouraged. Formal reviews tend to take place at key milestones and at the end of projects. As a consequence, one of the first steps in ensuring high quality feedback is to establish an end point in the work you are undertaking.

At first glance, it may seem strange to include a section within this chapter on bringing projects to a close, as surely it should be obvious when a project reaches its conclusion. However, this is one of the areas where external consultants have the advantage over Internal Consultants. For them, the end of a project is signalled by either delivering a final piece of work or being paid for the final time. For Internal Consultants and Business Partners, however, their continued presence in the business can mean that the end point is less clearly defined. A key part of their role is therefore to signal completion on a particular piece of work to their client, in order that it can be thoroughly reviewed and so that they can move on to something new and of more value.

Reviewing performance can take a number of different forms including:

- Self-reviews
- Client–Partner relationship reviews
- Feedback from the client system
- Project process reviews
- Business Partner Function reviews

Each of these is examined within this chapter and provides vital data for enhancing the performance of both the Business Partner and the Business as a whole.

Recognising the Need for Closure

One of the hardest parts for Internal Consultants is to recognise the end point and the need for closure on a particular project for themselves. If Business Partners are working effectively then at the end of their project the ownership should lie with the client and it should be straightforward to draw a line under the project and move on. However, for internal Business Partners this is fraught with difficulties as the Partner is keen to ensure that the relationship is sustained, and one way to do this is to help out with extra little tasks that need doing or by providing expertise when requested at key meetings or events. The client may be equally keen for the relationship to continue in this way, as it may provide an extra free resource!

If the project has been carefully monitored and progress has been tracked against a plan, it will be apparent when the tasks have been completed. However, there may still be some lingering activities that require your attention, or it may be 'easier' for the client or people in the client system to ask you to assist them in something rather than doing it themselves or through newly established processes. It is essential that the Business Partner continually asks themselves, 'Am I still adding value?' or 'Am I just carrying on to meet my own needs?' If you truly do feel your presence is still necessary on the project, then there is a need to re-negotiate an extended contract with your client, or set some new terms of reference to cover a transitional period. If not, then you need to be assertive with your client to clarify your current priorities with them. The ability to say no to your client when necessary has already been discussed in earlier chapters and is equally critical in the later stages of a project if you are to maintain your credibility.

Moving On from a Project Without Impacting the Relationship

Business Partners are human beings, and it is human nature to feel wanted. Ending a project, particularly a significant one, can leave you with a sense of loss and concern that important relationships may come to an end. Where the Business Partner model is based on the individual gaining their own work, there will also be added concerns that losing contact with your client may lead to a loss of further work. It is essential therefore that the Business Partner ends each project professionally and takes steps to continue to build on the relationships that have been established. Just because a project comes to an end, it should not mean that key contacts are lost, although it will mean that the nature of the relationship will need to change. The networking skills outlined in Part 2 will come into play as a means of maintaining relationships, as relationships are an area that needs to be actively managed to ensure success in the role.

Guidelines for Moving On

There are a number of steps a Business Partner can take to ease the transition at the end of a piece of work. Each of these will help to transfer the ownership of the project back to the client system and should ensure that the client is fully equipped to take on the different aspects of their role. This process is often referred to in consultancy terms as disengaging.

Establish the process at the start of the contract
It is essential that Business Partners establish a plan for disengaging early in the project. At the initial contracting phase, the Partner needs to be working with the client to establish:

- When each aspect of the project will be completed
- Who will be responsible for what at completion
- Any ongoing support that may be required after completion
- How the project will be reviewed

Some companies we spoke to, such as *Royal Bank of Scotland*, formally disengage from a major project by signing off an agreement that the initial terms of reference have been met. They then set up a maintenance contract, if required, to cover any ongoing support that is needed.

Incorporate symbols of completion
Holding certain events or providing awards can be a useful signal to the client that the project is coming to an end. Celebrating the success of a project is a helpful acknowledgement of completion and is useful

for both the client and the Business Partner in terms of cementing their relationship and demonstrating their value. This does not need to be overly formal, and as one Business Partner we spoke to put it 'I drag them (the client) down the pub whenever I've done anything I want to show off about!'.

Carrying out a thorough review of the project and the Partnership are also useful symbols of completion. This will allow for the Partner to formalise any ongoing support which may be needed, and depending on the original terms of reference it may also be necessary to produce a written report that needs to be signed off by the client.

More subtle signals can also be appropriate, such as a gradual spacing out of meetings or contact, or where cross-payment is made, a reduction in the percentage charged towards the end of a project.

Identify the right time

It can be useful for a Business Partner to ask themselves, 'Am I still adding value?' Although it is often nice to be working with a good client and feeling valued by them, Partners may have an increased sense that they are not doing anything the client group cannot do for themselves. At this time, done properly, Partners will enhance their credibility by stepping out of the project.

Ensure you follow-up

It is critical that Partners maintain the relationship they have built with the client group, so whilst they need to be clear that their role in the project is ending, they should also find ways to keep the contact going to continue the relationship. Follow-up dates are very useful not only in reviewing the project, but also as a way of legitimising continued personal contact with the client and key stakeholders.

Reviewing the Effectiveness of the Client–Partner Relationship

The end of a project is a good time to review your effectiveness as a Business Partner. In addition to evaluating the success of a particular project, which is discussed in more detail in the next chapter, it can also be an ideal time to review the effectiveness of your relationship with the client. Where you have a constant client within the business, the appraisal process may also provide an established review point, as is the case within *Barclays* and the *Inland Revenue*. In the Inland Revenue the customer's account managers establish a customer agreement at the start of each project and when the project is completed they evaluate the performance of the consulting Partner as part of their performance appraisal.

The review is likely to cover a number of different aspects, depending on the length and complexity of the Partnership project. In many organisations, such as the *BBC*, the process starts with a self-assessment, sometimes with the aid of a tick-box questionnaire. The questionnaire is also given to the client to complete and is used as a framework for the discussion which follows. Generally, reviews take place in a number of different ways which include:

- Self-reviews – assessing your own performance
- Client feedback
- Feedback from the client system
- Project process reviews
- Business Partner Function reviews
- Project outcome reviews (discussed in Chapter 10).

Assessing your own performance

The Business Partner behaviours, outlined in Part 2, provide a useful frame for assessing performance, from both your own and the client's perspective. The behavioural framework has been adapted into an assessment questionnaire outlined in the Appendix. Many organisations we spoke to had established competency frameworks that were used for self-assessment in a similar way.

Thomas and Elbeik (1996) also provide some useful checklists for carrying out a review of your own performance as an Internal Consultant. Some of the key questions which they suggest are useful to reflect on include:

- To what extent were the original goals met?
- Did the project stay within budget?
- Was the project delivered on time?
- What did I do well on this project?
- What would I do differently if I were to do it again?
- How effective was my relationship with the client?

- Was I always open and honest in my dealings?
- Have I left a positive impression with my client?
- What elements of this project can I use as an example of best practice?

Assessment from the client system

The client system includes not just the client themselves, but also other members of the project team, customers, sponsors, other stakeholders and key contacts throughout the project. There are advantages in gaining feedback on the relationship as well as the project. It can often help the Partner's credibility by admitting that their approach was not perfect and establish a firmer foundation for future work together.

Many organisations, such as *Royal and Sun Alliance*, use 360-degree feedback to provide data from a wider source within the client system. However, often more valuable than a questionnaire is the opportunity to hold structured interviews with the client system. Particular questions which could form the basis of a structured interview are:

- What do they see as my main contribution to the project?
- What specific actions helped in meeting the project goals?
- What specific actions hindered or delayed meeting the project goals?
- What could I have done differently to be more effective?
  - How proactive was I?
  - How prompt was I in dealing with queries?
  - How professional was I?
  - Were there any aspects I needed to understand better?
- How effective was the communication between us?
  - Did we have good rapport?
  - Did we have a high level of trust?
  - Was I listening as well as I could?
- Was the level of involvement appropriate?
- Did my service provide value for money?
- Would they recommend me for other projects?
- How could I do a better job if we were to work together again?

A visual continuum is another good way for a Business Partner to understand whether they are achieving the right balance in their approach to the client relationship. An example of the types of scales that might be appropriate are shown in Table 9.1.

Table 9.1 Client rating scale

Business Partner is ...		Business Partner is ...
Challenging	├─┼─┼─┼─┼─┼─┼─┼─┼─┤	Accepting
Clear	├─┼─┼─┼─┼─┼─┼─┼─┼─┤	Unclear
Practical	├─┼─┼─┼─┼─┼─┼─┼─┼─┤	Theoretical
Provides value for money	├─┼─┼─┼─┼─┼─┼─┼─┼─┤	Over priced
Open and friendly	├─┼─┼─┼─┼─┼─┼─┼─┼─┤	Distant and defensive
Trustworthy and honest	├─┼─┼─┼─┼─┼─┼─┼─┼─┤	Not to be trusted
Efficient with time	├─┼─┼─┼─┼─┼─┼─┼─┼─┤	Wastes time
Develops joint solutions	├─┼─┼─┼─┼─┼─┼─┼─┼─┤	Imposes solutions
Credible	├─┼─┼─┼─┼─┼─┼─┼─┼─┤	Lacking in confidence
Willing to adapt and change	├─┼─┼─┼─┼─┼─┼─┼─┼─┤	Inflexible/resistant
A true partner	├─┼─┼─┼─┼─┼─┼─┼─┼─┤	Unequal partner

Reviewing the Effectiveness of the Project

In addition to reviewing the effectiveness of the relationship between the Business Partner and the client, there is also benefit to be gained from reviewing the way the project was managed. Often these discussions can get mixed together. Whilst this is sometimes inevitable, it can be hugely advantageous to separate the two, to prevent the discussion taking a bias towards either the relationship or the project issues. Particular interventions or projects will benefit from having their own review process, in terms of the quality and the approach used. This is different again from evaluating the outcomes of a particular project, which is discussed in the next chapter.

It is good practice to produce either a written or a verbal report at the end of each project, as this then provides a structured method for conducting a review, as well as symbolising the end of your involvement in the project to the client. The review can cover a number of different aspects, depending on the length and complexity of the

Partnership project. Completing a 'learning log' as you progress through the project may help with the review.

The review of the project may contain:

- A review of project effectiveness that is, did it meet the outcomes intended?
    - Has it delivered the intended benefits?
    - Has the original problem been addressed?
- A review of the process effectiveness
    - What helped the project go smoothly?
    - Were the right people involved?
    - How effective was the communication?
    - How effective was the planning?
    - What got in the way of progress?
    - What should we do differently next time?
- A review of project and process efficiency
- Customer satisfaction
    - What do you like about the outcome?
    - What are you not so sure about?
    - Have you experienced any further problems?
    - What further changes or additions would you recommend?
- Client/others reporting on the project
    Sometimes the client may need help to recognise different stakeholders' perspectives on the project and it may be appropriate to gather data from a range of sources.

This review process is not intended to evaluate the business impact, but will provide useful data to enhance the service provided.

Utilising feedback

If you follow the guidelines set out in this chapter then you will gain a lot of information about yourself, your client and stakeholder's perceptions of you and the effectiveness of the processes that were used. However this is not the final step, as it is essential that this information does not disappear into a vacuum, never to be referred to again. Some of the Business Partners we spoke to said 'I wish I could find more time for proper reviews', but unless you prioritise your time to incorporate reviews then it is unlikely you will be enhancing your performance at an optimum rate.

The data needs to be utilised in some way to enhance the service provided and your own performance. Carrying out a mini-diagnostic study on your own feedback will provide you with the insights needed to decide what actions to take forward in the future.

Members of CIPD can use the data to review their Continued Professional Development (CPD) and establish new learning targets. More importantly, credibility with clients and key stakeholders can be hugely increased by demonstrating learning from the feedback, and working in different ways with people as a result of the learning.

Reviewing the Effectiveness of the Business Partnership Function

It may also be appropriate for the Business Partnership Function to review its own position from time to time and get together as a team to analyse the areas they want and need to improve the most.

Table 9.2 provides a set of questions which provide a basis for a functional review. This can be completed either together as a team or individually, and the results compared.

Table 9.2   Review of the Business Partnership Function

Rate each of the following factors according to how you perceive the Business Partner Function meets the criteria given	Score between 1–10 1 = Poor; 5 = OK; 10 = Excellent
Business credibility 1. Understanding of the business needs 2. Credibility with Line Managers 3. Perceived level of Customer Service 4. Sufficient budget/resource to meet needs 5. Relationships with key stakeholders 6. Brand image 7. Broad network across all areas	

(Continued)

193

Table 9.2 Review of the Business Partnership Function—Cont'd

Rate each of the following factors according to how you perceive the Business Partner Function meets the criteria given	Score between 1–10 1 = Poor; 5 = OK; 10 = Excellent

Future focus
  8. Understanding of the challenges facing the company
  9. Priorities are towards the longer-term company goals
 10. Involvement in strategic discussions
 11. Linkage of HR activities to Business Challenges

Business Partner teamwork
 12. Sharing best practice and transferring knowledge
 13. Celebrating success
 14. Building skills and knowledge

Even without such a formal review, posing questions for discussion at team meetings such as

- What are the greatest challenges facing the organisation at the moment and are we partnering in those areas?
- How strong is our brand image within the organisation?
- What can we do to improve our network?

can be a useful stimulus for ideas and a focus for developing the function as a whole.

Reviewing priorities

Business Partner Functions are faced with a myriad of choices about how they spend their time and focus their energy. Key challenges mentioned by Business Partners we spoke to included:

- Culture change
- Re-engineering HR processes

- Communication
- Employee relations issues
- Skills training
- Redeployment
- Executive coaching
- Cross-functional working
- Technology integration
- Performance management
- Competency development
- Motivation and morale
- Mentoring
- Mergers and acquisitions
- Structural changes – centralising/decentralising
- Reward changes
- Skills shortages
- Downsizing
- Partnerships
- Outsourcing
- Diversity
- Absenteeism.

To name but a few!

It also would not be a surprise if you are reading this list and thinking 'all of these and more!'. So if Business Partners are working on many of these issues, it is critical that the function as a whole creates some definition of the key strategic objectives and prioritises the business needs, as discussed in Chapter 2.

Many tools exist to help define key strategic objectives for organisations, such as McKinsey's 7S model (Peters et al., 1980) as well as SWOT and PEST analyses. McKinsey's model (Figure 9.1) helps to review whether the individual strategies for different areas of the business are mutually supportive. For example, do the systems in place relate to the structure and values the organisation is seeking to achieve? Does the style of managers reflect the needs of the business?

Turbo Charging the HR function (Mooney, 2001) also has a useful 'Strategic Clarity Quiz' for assessing whether you are as clear as you think you are on the business strategy. The book also suggests you ask

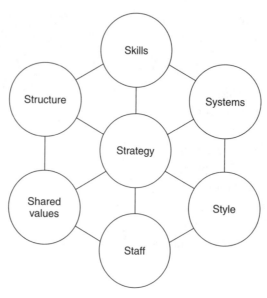

Figure 9.1 McKinsey's 7S model

yourself whether you would feel capable of giving a talk to new recruits on the organisational strategy, which is a good indicator of your understanding. However, one model which can be particularly useful for reviewing priorities is to link the HR activity to the business life cycle and the stage of organisational development. Table 9.3 illustrates the stages of business development linked to the key HR challenges.

Table 9.3 HR priorities linked to the stage of organisational development

	Staffing	Rewards	Training	Employee relations	Goals cultural
Start up	Key skills	Salary equity	Key skills	Philosophy	Flexibility
Growth	Skills mix	Salary bonuses	Skills building	Commitment	Growth
Maturity	Retention of key players	Focus on efficiency	Management skills	Involvement	Efficiency Motivation
Decline	Redeployment	Focus on cost-saving	Retraining	Flexibility	Cost reduction

It may be that in large corporations, different business areas have very different priorities as they are at differing stages of development. Business Partners in *Marconi*, for example, are largely focused on initiatives aimed at cost reduction and effective redeployment of staff as some of the areas of their business move into decline. Other developing areas, however, require a focus on building new skills.

Summary

Reviewing your performance as a Business Partner is an essential and often neglected part of the role. The information you can glean from taking time out to reflect on your performance and gather data from those around you can be invaluable in terms of providing new insights and learning to enable you to enhance your performance. Not only that, but the process of gathering the data can also help to build more solid relationships with those around you, particularly if you ensure that you act on the information you receive.

Often the difficulty in reviewing progress comes from Business Partners inability to detach themselves from particular pieces of work and clearly signalling to their client that their involvement has ended. Contracting effectively and incorporating symbols to indicate completion can help with this process.

Questioning is a vital skill of any Business Partner and this chapter contains many suggested questions to assess performance by both yourself and others. More important than the questions themselves, however, is the way in which the information gleaned is used and the useful dialogues that asking such searching questions can lead you into.

Reviewing the Business Partnership Function as a whole is also critical not only in ensuring that Business Partners are working in a co-ordinated way and are sharing knowledge and skills, but also to ensure the right business focus. Establishing clear priorities for the function based on the business needs is imperative if Business Partners are to stay focused on work that adds value rather than just pleasing their clients. The HR priorities need to be aligned to the strategic and cultural objectives of the organisation, as well as the stage of development the company has reached.

Checklist

- Am I continually reviewing whether I am adding value to this project?
- Do I feel as if I am still holding the client or consumer's hand for my own benefit or for their benefit?
- Have I taken steps to signal the end of a particular project to the client?
- How do I review my own performance as a Business Partner?
- Is there a clear and effective process for reviewing the effectiveness of my relationship with the client?
- Is there a clear and effective process for reviewing each project?
- Are the customers and other stakeholders involved in any review?
- Do I make time to make sense of the feedback and analyse the data?
- Am I demonstrating learning and applying new ways of working as a result of the review process?
- What processes are in place for reviewing the effectiveness of the Business Partnership Function as a whole?
- How well are the priorities of the Partnership Function aligned with the business needs?

References

Mooney, P. (2001) *Turbo Charging the HR Function*, Chartered Institute of Personnel and Development, London.

Peters, T., Philips, J. and Waterman R. McKinsey (1980) 'Structure is not Organisation', *Business Horizons*, Vol. 23, June, pp.14–26.

Thomas, M. and Elbeik, S. (1996) *Supercharge Your Management Role: Making the Transition to Internal Consultant*, Butterworth-Heinemann, Oxford.

10

Measuring Your Impact

Many of you, I feel sure, will have turned to this chapter with the hope of finding an easy solution as to how to measure the success of HR when working as Business Partners. Yet interestingly, in all the research which took place for this book, very few of the organisations we spoke to were taking any active steps at all to measure their effectiveness, beyond evaluating the delivery of specific projects. So do you need to bother measuring your impact? And if so, how do you go about doing it?

Evaluating the Success of the Partnership

Unless the Partnership Function is still being established, one of the key questions facing Business Partnerships is 'How can I show the Business Partnership Function adds value?' As pressures on businesses increase and there is a continual need to justify costs, there is likely to come a time when Business Partners need to invest some of their time justifying their own existence. If a Partnership project goes well then there will be a sense of satisfaction and verbal recognition from the client that the Business Partnership has been of value, but this is rarely enough in today's world of constant justification of costs within the business. Business Partners need to take more active steps to ensure that they are constantly demonstrating value for money.

The shift from Operational HR to Strategic HR partnerships has meant that traditional measures of efficiency and effectiveness of HR processes are no longer appropriate. To demonstrate business improvement, Business Partners need to collect information which will show the added value the Partner is having on the business and their strategic contribution. This, in turn, will help justify the function. The evaluation data can also be used to enhance the credibility of the function, by illustrating the work it undertakes and marketing the Business Partner role, using examples of past successes. If Business Partners are responsible for gaining business internally, this will be an essential marketing lever.

However, evaluation is not easy. Interestingly, in a recent study of HR evaluation practices, whilst the majority of Directors (95%) agreed that it was important to measure the strategic impact of HR, only 40 per cent believed it was possible to do so, and this lack of knowledge about *how* to approach evaluation is a key deterrent to any evaluation taking place at all (Cabrera, 2003). It is evident that organisations struggle to evaluate the organisational impact of change processes effectively and with ever-increasing pressures on time and resources, success is often seen as stemming from a lack of negative feedback rather than real added value to the business. Yet the pressure on internal service departments to evaluate the impact they have on the business is growing and for HR Business Partners this is no longer about what they do, but whether they deliver business improvement.

One of the possible reasons for the increased pressure on HR to evaluate is the number of companies seeking to obtain accreditation for Investors in People (IIP). Achieving IIP status has become a prestigious achievement for many organisations and for HR moving towards a Business Partnership model, achieving IIP is almost essential. The IIP framework is based around four principles, the fourth of which is evaluation of the business benefits. IIP is a total quality framework and works on the premise that evaluation sits in a cycle of planning, doing, evaluating and reviewing. Whilst there is limited guidance on evaluation methodologies, the need to evaluate as part of the IIP standard has been significant and 45 per cent of organisations cite this as a prime reason for carrying out evaluation (Industrial Society, 2000).

Very few of the organisations carrying out evaluation, however, do so in a way which determines the business impact. Traditionally, Training and Development functions have the most expertise within HR for evaluating their success. However, if Business Partnerships follow the trend set by training functions then it makes sorry reading, as the training in a Britain survey estimated that only 19 per cent of organisations try to evaluate the business benefits of training and only 3 per cent of those attempt any sort of cost/benefit analysis.

This chapter will examine how Business Partners can seek to establish better processes for measuring their success and will review some of the more traditional as well as emerging models for evaluation, in order to give an insight into the variety of approaches on offer.

What Gets in the Way?

If the pressure to evaluate is getting stronger and the benefits of evaluating are evident, it is worth starting out by looking at what gets in the way of effective evaluations. Even when there is a clear intent on the part of the Business Partner and the client to evaluate the project, there are immense pressures within the organisation, which run counter to any meaningful evaluation taking place.

Time

At the end of a project, the pressure is often on to finish quickly and move on to the next job. The client is likely to lose focus and a sense of priority towards a task nearing completion and be motivated to 'not waste time' discussing it. This is particularly the case if the project went very well or very badly. In order to overcome this, the Business Partner needs to make sure they have an earlier agreement to evaluate and review, which they can refer back to, as well as the courage of their convictions in pressing for the review to take place. Being clear of the benefits in your own mind is imperative if you are to overcome resistance from the client, as is the need to have contracted some time up front to carry out the review.

Events have changed

During a lengthy Partnership project, the chances are that significant organisational changes will be taking place alongside the work being undertaken. More frequently than ever before, companies are re-structuring, downsizing, de-layering, revising working practices and bringing in new technologies. It is all too easy to get to the end of a project and agree with the client that 'things have moved on' and that attempting to draw a line between the outcome and the starting point are now inappropriate, despite good intentions at the start. Once again, contracting and re-contracting throughout the project are imperative to prevent this happening.

Inappropriate measures

What is valued in organisations is often what is already being measured and reported. Linking in with these measures can therefore be highly beneficial for Business Partners, as they will not have to collect new data and will be working with established reports. However, many of the measures existing in organisations focus on 'hard' rather than 'soft' data and even where hard measures change, it is often difficult to produce evidence about how the Partnership intervention impacted the change. Business Partners therefore need to be careful to choose measures that are both relevant and easily attainable in the business.

The need to focus on 'quick wins'

At the start of any Business Partnership there is a pressure to establish your credibility by delivering quickly and effectively in a number of areas. The investment of time is viewed as better placed on meeting the client's current needs rather than following up the outcomes of previous work. Whilst this is a good model to follow in some ways, it does have the consequence that a pattern is being established whereby it becomes normal practice not to build in a process for review and evaluation. Many Business Partners we spoke to said that they would like to carry out more evaluation but at the current time the focus needed to be on delivery, as a means of establishing themselves in the Partnership role. Having established themselves as a Partner who delivers without taking time to review, however, it will be difficult to reverse this mould once the Partner is more established, as the client's expectations will already be set.

Good Practice Guidelines for Establishing a Focus on Evaluation

So what can Business Partners do to prevent this happening? As a first step, Business Partners need to ensure that they focus their role towards evaluation. This is not as easy as it sounds, but if Partners hold certain principles in mind throughout their role then it should be possible to achieve this. Listed below are a number of good practice guidelines which are aimed at establishing an appropriate focus on the evaluation process.

Good practice guidelines:

- Do not partner for the sake of it
- Set measures and contract up front
- Assess the time frames
- Choose your measures carefully
- Continually involve your client
- Let the client take the credit
- Separate out validation from evaluation
- Choose an appropriate level for analysis.

Do not partner for the sake of it

When you first get involved in a Business Partnership project, there needs to be some assessment of the importance of the project and its impact on the organisation. Through careful questioning, the Partner should be able to glean whether the proposal is critical to the business, important to the business or more administrative. Paul Kearns (2001) shows where an effective Business Partnership Function should be operating (Figure 10.1).

Even if a Business Partnership appears very attractive (perhaps due to lack of other business or a desire to work with a particular client), in order to sustain credibility and value, Business Partners should not accept work that is not going to add value to the business. If they do, then the evaluation phase will be an unwelcome addition to the process for the Business Partner, as it will more than likely show that they achieved little more than building a new relationship!

When *Coca-Cola* first repositioned their HR function as a Business Partnership, one of their first steps was to identify criteria to evaluate the work they were asked to do (Brocket, 2004). In true Partnership style, they involved business managers to help develop criteria which they then used to identify the relative importance of HR projects. The criteria they developed were that the work:

1. Contributes to business performance
2. Promotes early delivery of business benefits
3. Maximises employee engagement
4. Improves or simplifies people management activities
5. Supports legal or regulatory compliance.

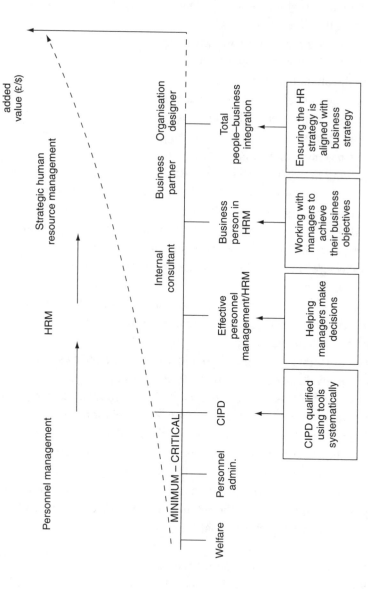

Figure 10.1 Moving up the HR ROI scale

Source: Kearns (2001), Copyright by Paul Kearns

Each of these criteria was given a weighting, and existing projects were ranked against this in order to prioritise the HR project portfolio.

This type of approach provides a clear understanding of why the Partnership is taking place and what the areas of impact a particular piece of work is predicted to have. If there is not a strong priority for a particular project, this will be clear from the outset.

Set measures and contract up front

Although evaluation is often left to the end, it cannot be stressed enough that, to be effective, measures need to be discussed and agreed at the contracting phase. It is much easier to carry out a thorough review if there is buy-in up front and time has been allocated to it at the start of the project. For example, *Frizzell* go through an explicit process of 'contracting' with the line, where programmes are devised and prioritised against the business needs and strategy. This makes it much easier to assess whether those business needs were met at completion.

As discussed in previous chapters, the purpose of the initial contracting discussions is to ensure that the customer's requirements are accurately translated into actions by the Business Partner, and have measurable outcomes. As with any good project management processes, it is important to get the scope and specification right before committing the necessary resource. It not only conveys a professional image to the internal customer, but also allows misunderstandings to be picked up at an early stage. Some external consultancies, such as *Leaps and Bounds*, are paid on achieving the success measures set up front and this provides a useful focus for their activity. This model could usefully be transferred to internal partnerships.

Although the measures are ideally agreed up front, there also needs to be flexibility and the measures should be continually reviewed. The Partner needs to be continually asking 'what does success look like for you?' so that as the project progresses the appropriateness of the original success measures are challenged and re-contracted if necessary.

Assess the time frames

It is important to evaluate within the frame that is given for a particular project, rather than an ideal position. If, for example, a project is only given six months to run, when both the Partner and the client agree that eight months would ensure the quality outcome required, then the measures should be set to reflect the shorter timescales.

However, much strategic HR activity has a longer payback period than the Partnership project is likely to last. Work on a new succession planning process, for example, will typically not show its true value until some years after being put in place. In these cases, it is recommended that the risk of not taking any action is built into the cost analysis. In this example, that would mean costing delays in recruitment to key positions, or assessing the predicted impact on turnover. Softer measures may also be more appropriate, such as the level of awareness of the new process amongst key managers.

Choose your measures carefully

Carrying out evaluation overtly carries a strong message. The questions you choose to ask will give a strong message in themselves about what you are really aiming to achieve. Measuring the quantity of sales calls and not the quality of the calls, for example, will indicate that the intervention is aiming to improve efficiency, possibly at the expense of effectiveness.

Effective Partners will discuss with their clients the impact of choosing particular measures and will ask probing questions to ensure the client has a clear understanding of what they are aiming to achieve with the evaluation.

Typical questions might include:

- How engaged or active do you want to be?
- How much risk are you willing to take?
- Who should set the standards and measures?
- How are they going to be used?
- What message do these measures send?

Continually involve your client

Abernathy (1999) makes an important point when he says 'any good manager knows how her work unit is performing and is paid to make some well-informed judgements about what's causing the performance to change'. Some organisations have had a lot of success by discarding formal evaluation processes and using line manager's perceptions on the impact of change.

Whether you take this approach or not, you will want to get you internal customer involved in the process of establishing measures as early as possible in the project. It can be useful to get their agreement on the benchmarks and measures you are going to use and also establish when and how the results will be tracked. It is also worth discussing any variables which may affect the outcome of the project, so that causal links can be established.

Many Business Partners also choose to seek feedback from other parts of the client system, such as the stakeholders, customers, people involved in the data gathering process, etc. Surveys and focus groups are common methods used for this process. However, the Partner needs to be wary of creating a project in itself from the evaluation. The extent of the feedback needs to be appropriate and not overly time-consuming and it is therefore important to balance the need for feedback with the cost of gaining it. Evaluators need to work as 'real partners' with other managers in the organisation to gain a greater understanding of the relevant performance measures and the causal links.

Let the client take the credit

If you are good at what you do, it is often said that the client will think that they were responsible for it happening. Working as internal partners, the satisfaction comes from client satisfaction and watching change projects become institutionalised into the new culture and organisation. The word-of-mouth recommendations and demand for your services are the credit you receive from a job well done and these allow you access to more interesting projects and areas of the organisation.

Separate out validation from evaluation

There are many things that can be measured and reviewed within the scope of a Business Partnership and it is important to be clear with your client and yourself on what you are seeking to achieve at any one time. It can be helpful to differentiate between *validation*, which is concerned with whether the intervention or process achieved what it set out to do, and *evaluation*, which focuses on the impact of that intervention on individuals and the business. Validation is therefore more about the quality and appropriateness of what went on, and evaluation is more about results. Both of these approaches are likely to have value.

Choose an appropriate level for analysis

Business Partners need to work with their constraints and opportunities to use evaluation tools to best effect. It is important to clarify why the information is being collected and what use will be made of it. Different types of evaluation can then be used, depending on the nature, scope and purposes of evaluating the intervention. Gathering customised data can be a time-consuming business, and the level of the analysis needs to reflect the size of the project and the likely benefits of demonstrating bottom-line results.

Certainly companies with comprehensive evaluation processes such as *IBM*, *Motorola* and *Arthur Anderson* evaluate in response to customer needs rather than to justify the activity or maintain a budget. At Arthur Anderson bottom-line results were measured less than 10 per cent of the time, but the studies were very useful to them in increasing customer confidence generally. Business Partners can therefore benefit from choosing where to place their effort in terms of evaluation and not investing unreasonable amounts of time proving business benefits for every piece of work they are involved in.

Make it worth your while!

Anyone who has tried to do a comprehensive evaluation of an HR project will be aware that it is a time-consuming and frustrating activity. Even when measures are discussed and agreed up front, the changing nature of the business can make it difficult to establish causal links. In my experience, no Business Partner in their right mind is likely to embark on evaluating a piece of work unless there is an incentive for them to do so. However, if it is something you believe is necessary then establishing evaluation as one of your key performance indicators is one way of encouraging activity in this area. Given that the whole purpose of Business Partners is to have an impact on the business, financial rewards based on business improvement are also worth considering.

What Models of Evaluation Might Apply to Business Partnerships?

HR working as Business Partners is a relatively new discipline and as such there are few established models for evaluating success. In drawing together approaches which are talked about for this chapter, it became apparent that the models used stem from a number of different areas, each of which has a value to bring to the process. Figure 10.2 highlights some of the key models in existence, each of which will be discussed in turn.

Traditional HR approaches

Benchmarking
Balanced scorecard
Satisfaction surveys
Activity tracking

Evaluation options

OD models

Kirkpatrick's four levels
KPMT model
Responsive evaluation

Emerging Business Partner models

Figure 10.2   Evaluation models

Traditional HR Approaches

Historically, as HR has focused more on transactional activities such as hiring, firing and administering rewards, the common approach to measuring the value of HR has focused on evaluating HR as a profit centre. The tools most useful for this type of evaluation are:

- Satisfaction surveys
- Balanced scorecard
- Benchmarking
- Activity tracking.

Whilst these methods may still have their uses, if HR is working as a true Business Partner then the focus needs to move away from analysing HR transactions to measuring improvements in business results.

Employee satisfaction surveys

Opinion or satisfaction surveys provide a measurable trend on HR issues and are commonplace in large organisations. Research shows that levels of employee satisfaction have a direct correlation with business performance, so monitoring changes in the level of satisfaction can be a useful indicator.

Surveys can also be important for Business Partners as a way of tracking cultural change in areas such as communication, employee issues and perceptions of customer service. The possible disadvantage of focusing on survey improvements as a way of measuring success for HR is that what employees rate poorly becomes the focus for HR projects, rather than necessarily focusing on what adds value to the business.

The balanced scorecard

The balanced scorecard model, developed by Kaplan and Norton (1996), provides a means of measuring and tracking the impact of employee-related initiatives on the bottom line. It has been widely adopted in organisations, including *BNFL*, *Royal and Sun Alliance* and the *CAA*.

Typically, it looks at results from the perspective of:

- Finance (e.g. revenue growth and cost improvements)
- Customer (e.g. satisfaction measures, market share)
- Internal business processes (e.g. operational efficiency)
- Learning and growth (e.g. employee satisfaction, skill levels).

The specific measures an organisation includes in its scorecard vary depending on the nature of the business and its strategic approach, but are intended to give a more holistic sense of how the business is performing. Typical HR measures include compensation and benefits, recruitment, absenteeism, turnover, training and development, and health and safety.

External benchmarking

A benchmark is a standard against which items can be compared. It helps to determine how the company or function is performing compared to other organisations in similar sectors as well as providing models of best practice. Benchmarking is ideally an ongoing process of measuring practices and procedures against competitors or those considered best in class in order to give an indication of where improvements can be made.

In terms of HR, benchmarking data is often gathered on:

- Ratio of HR to managers in the organisation
- Board membership and levels of HR staff

- HR processes
- HR structure and functions
- Turnover rates
- Use of technology by HR
- Training provision
- Evaluation practices.

Benchmarking Business Partnership Functions may also lead to gathering data on:

- The perceived image of the department or section
- The cost charging mechanism
- The ratio of Partners to managers in the organisation
- Qualification levels of Business Partners
- Added-value data.

One of the difficulties with benchmarking is that it can be hard to identify appropriate companies as comparators and each company will place a different emphasis on particular aspects of HR depending on how they connect to the business. It is important that when looking for benchmarking data checks are made on whether the data is current and whether it measures the same things you want to measure.

In large, diverse organisations, internal benchmarking may also be appropriate, in order to compare the success of the Partnership Function in different areas. This can help to improve internal best practice and make knowledge transfer more effective. The Partnership Function within the *Inland Revenue*, for example, came up against barriers within the business over whether they added value. They chose to use benchmarking across organisations to help to show their worth.

Activity tracking/HR costing

In this method, the value of the HR function is determined by the level of activity, such as the number of new employees recruited in a period of time. The cost of each activity is measured and tracked as a way of identifying areas where savings can be made. This type of process is more appropriate for transactional HR and is less applicable for Business Partnership models as it assumes that HR activity adds value, without establishing links to the business results.

OD Evaluation Models

Many of the processes for evaluating internal consultancy are drawn from models used for training and development. Highlighted below are some of the key models in existence which are seen to have application in Business Partnerships projects. More detail on these and other OD methods can be found in Tamkin, Yarnall and Kerrin (2002). These models indicate that there is a need to focus more clearly on the different types of outcomes sought by the interventions and to tailor the technique to the organisation in order to ensure that the approach suits the culture and values. In addition, there is an increased emphasis on non-financial measures and a suggestion that a more rounded picture needs to be developed to show the indirect returns on all aspects of the business.

The four-level approach – Kirkpatrick

The best-known and most widely used framework for classifying evaluation is the Kirkpatrick model (Kirkpatrick, 1996). Benchmarking forums have shown that Kirkpatrick's model of evaluation is still the predominant means of evaluating OD. Where this model is used, more and more companies, such as *BT*, are also attempting to evaluate certain key activities at the higher levels of application of learning and impact on the organisation. Although Kirkpatrick's model has come under some criticisms in recent years, the strengths of the model lie in its simplicity and pragmatic way of helping practitioners think about interventions.

The model consists of four stages, described more recently by Kirkpatrick as levels. Each of these four levels is examined critically below:

Level 1: Reaction

This assesses what the participants thought of a particular intervention, and is normally assessed by the use of reaction questionnaires.

Gathering data at a reaction level can help to assess the initial impact of an intervention and can have real value in terms of encouraging a positive message and giving an indication of teething problems in terms of either method or content. A recent study by the Industrial Society found that 84 per cent of companies evaluate reactions to training and development using reaction questionnaires or 'reaction-naires' (Industrial Society, 2000). Yet despite this, there is considerable evidence to suggest that reaction-level evaluation has little value in terms of determining business impact.

In a training context it has been found that participants' reactions were generally unrelated to subsequent job behaviour (Warr et al., 1999) and this finding is backed up by other researchers who also found negative relationships between reactions and learning – that is, if the participants found the intervention uncomfortable and unsettling, it may have had more impact on them than they were prepared to admit (Alliger and Janak, 1989).

One reason for this may be that learners often mistake good presentation style as good learning, and difficult messages may lead to poor ratings. Psychologists have argued that people are not good at reporting their experiences and many people argue against participants evaluating training instructors for this reason, as the evaluation data may lead to inappropriate changes to the training programme. This would also be relevant to Business Partners choosing to evaluate the reactions to interventions they make.

As a result, if Business Partners choose to use reaction-level measures to assess their intervention, they need to analyse quite carefully the types of reactions they are assessing and be clear about the purpose of the data. The evidence suggests that if organisations are seeking to evaluate the *value* of the intervention rather than aiming to improve on its content, then reaction data may not be appropriate. In addition, even when there is an interest in improving effectiveness by validating the intervention in terms of content and process, the literature suggests that data generated need to be treated with caution due to the inability of raters to distinguish impact from style or approach.

Level 2: Learning
Level 2 measures the changes in knowledge, skills or attitude with respect to the objectives of the intervention.

Where a Partnership intervention is aimed at changing knowledge, skills or attitude, this is normally assessed using some type of performance rating, or by participant and line manager giving feedback on the extent of the change taking place. There is a high level of agreement in

213

the literature that ideally measures of performance need to be taken both before and after the intervention to be able to assess the change. Control groups are commonly suggested as a good way of countering the effects of other factors which may affect the performance levels. Often however, testing prior to an event taking place and establishing control groups are not practical for organisations due to the numbers involved and organisational constraints. As a result the measures used are often less scientific.

In organisations, 360-degree assessment is growing in popularity and is one way of assessing competency gains over time. *Motorola*, for example, used 360-degree performance appraisal to measure leadership behaviours and looked at how this related to the training the leaders had received (Blanchard et al., 2000).

Level 3: Behaviour and the transfer of learning

Level 3 measures changes in job behaviour resulting from an intervention and seeks to identify whether the learning is being applied. Assessment methods typically include observation, self- and manager-assessments, and productivity data.

Organisational culture and the degree of management support for change have been shown to have a significant effect on the transfer of learning from behavioural change programmes to changed behaviour in the workplace. Research indicates that when supervisors and peers encourage and reward the application of new approaches, the intervention is likely to achieve more positive results. Business Partners can therefore take active steps to encourage management support and cultural change in line with projects being implemented.

Some of the important cultural elements which effect success at this level are an individual's 'self-efficacy', or the degree to which employees have confidence in their own ability to cope with new tasks, as well as an employee's motivation to learn and their willingness to put any new skills and knowledge into practice.

Level 4: Results

Level 4 measures the bottom-line contribution of interventions. Methods used for evaluation include measuring costs, quality and Return on Investment (ROI).

Are 'hard' measures always possible?

Certainly the premise of Business Partnership is based on the belief that interventions not linked to organisational mission, strategy and goals are unlikely to produce results that are valued by the organisation and that it should be possible to forecast the financial benefits before a project begins.

However, the process of linking HR interventions to business results is highly interpretative, especially in complex business environments. Pulley (1994) argues that what is needed is 'responsive evaluation' which pays attention to both hard and soft issues and provides both quantitative and qualitative measures. She states that relying too heavily on either type of data can result in misleading conclusions. She draws on research which shows that people's actions tend to be more affected by stories and anecdotes than statistical results and argues that although senior managers may request hard data, they are more influenced by qualitative measures.

The ability of 'hard' measures to become visible in an appropriate time frame is also questioned. Many researchers argue that organisational constraints impact on the rigour of evaluation and that whilst some measures and cross-validation can be achieved, the 'worth' of a project is not just about cost-benefit. Often it can take 12–18 months to establish evaluation data that proves the effectiveness of a particular intervention, and the time lag needs to be taken account of when relating results to the bottom line. Kaplan and Norton (1996) go further than this and argue that financial measures are inadequate for guiding and evaluating organisations. 'They are lagging indicators that fail to capture much of the value that has been created or destroyed by manager's actions in the accounting period.'

In addition, some transformational programmes aimed at shifting culture can often happen before the organisation is ready for them and consequently the benefits are not visible for some time after. Rough (1994) argues that progress sometimes needs to be based upon trust, mutual involvement and facilitation. The *Ministry of Defence* (2001) evaluation toolkit appears to take this approach and states that evidence of results can be direct, indirect, quantifiable or qualitative, as long as managers have a sufficient range of information with which to make a decision.

However, there is an increasing concern in organisations to justify investment in terms of improved organisational performance, such as increased productivity, profit or safety, reduced error and enhanced market share and there are a number of supporters of the view that results can and should be analysed using numerical 'hard' data. Many researchers in this area believe that all results can be turned into numerical measures and that every business has numerous hard indicators of organisational effectiveness at their disposal, such as manufacturing efficiency, inventory levels, accidents, order-entry accuracy, abandoned calls, defect rates and cycle times. Plenty of guidance is also available for practitioners for measuring productivity, cost-effectiveness and ROI. More recently the Watson Wyatt Human Capital Index has also established exactly which human-capital practices have the greatest impact on shareholder value (see Pfau and Cundiff, 2002).

The KPMT model – Kearns and Miller (1997)

Kearns and Miller argue that clear objectives are an essential component of an evaluation model. They have developed a useful 'toolkit' to help evaluators work through the process of identifying bottom-line objectives through questioning techniques; evaluating existing deliverables; and using process mapping to identify the added value to organisations.

They argue that interventions can bring added value to an organisation only if the business is not performing effectively or there is a market opportunity which can be exploited. There is a heavy emphasis on establishing measures up front and clarifying objectives from a business perspective rather than that of the participants.

The key elements cited prior to the start of the process involve a broader analysis of the organisational context – its values, practices and current situation. Following this, there is a more explicit focus on the needs of the business and how these tie to the development of objectives and the design of the most appropriate solution. Whilst not forming part of the assessment process, it is argued that these contextual steps inform the future evaluation strategy and as such need to be included in any evaluation model.

The process they suggest to achieve this is:

Step 1   Discuss the needs of the business
Step 2   Design some proposed training and development solutions

Step 3   Decide on the real training issues and get buy-in to this
Step 4   Deliver
Step 5   Evaluate
Step 6   Give feedback on the results.

Where Kearns and Miller differ from some of the other models is that they believe that ROI can only be looked at in hard terms. As an example, they argue that even if an intervention is aimed at bringing about greater awareness (e.g. of customers), it should still only be measured by the eventual effect on hard measures such as customer spend and number of customers.

Applying their model to Business Partnership, the percentage ROI for a particular project would be calculated as

$$\frac{\text{Benefits from intervention (\$)} - \text{Costs of intervention (\$)}}{\text{Costs of intervention (\$)}}$$

To combat the difficulties of attributing long-term financial gains directly to a particular intervention, they suggest the use of simple process-flow maps so that the causal connections can be made explicit.

Business Partners interested in this approach are recommended to read Paul Kearns' forthcoming book on evaluation and ROI and his more recent books in 2001 and 2003.

Responsive evaluation – Pulley (1994)
Responsive evaluation is a tool for communicating evaluation results more effectively by tailoring it to the needs of the decision-makers. Pulley argues that the objective of the evaluation should be to provide evidence so that key decision-makers can determine what they want to know. The stages involved are:

1. Identify the decision-makers so as to ascertain who will be using the information and what their stake in it is.
2. Identify the information needs of the decision-makers – what do they need to know and how will it influence their decisions?
3. Systematically collect both quantitative and qualitative data. Pulley argues that the qualitative data is normally relayed in the form of stories or anecdotes and 'gives life to the numbers'.

4. Translate the data into meaningful information.
5. Involve and inform decision-makers on an ongoing basis.

This technique may have a lot of relevance to the work of Business Partners, particularly where their role is less project-related. The approach would be to find out what your internal customers want in terms of success measures and then collect the data that will answer those questions, rather than be defined by a pre-existing framework.

Business Partnership Models

The aim of Business Partnership is to move away from operational delivery to impacting the business at a strategic level. By definition this means that evaluating HR activity or planned interventions is unlikely to provide an accurate picture of the impact Business Partners are having. Whilst there are a few studies that have shown that moving to a more strategic role in HR does impact the firm's performance (Becker and Huselid, 1998), there is little evidence of the particular activities that add value or of how to assess the value added.

Cabrera (2003) argues that evaluation needs to move away from traditional measures of HR and focus on the extent to which employee behaviours are contributing towards the organisation's strategic objectives and the extent to which existing HR practices are encouraging or discouraging the desired behaviours. For example, a high-tech company pursuing a strategy of innovation and speed of delivery to market will be seeking staff who are highly committed, creative, work in self-managed teams and are empowered to take risks. The Business Partner role should be focused in this instance on ensuring that the culture and nature of the employees are in line with this. Evaluating the success of the role is therefore focused on the links between what the Business Partner does, employee behaviours and the business results. Three relatively new models have emerged in the literature to support this role and each of these is examined below.

Herring (2001)

Herring discusses how HR can determine their 'market-value' by a five-step process. Once again, this approach has its basis in identifying up front what the key issues are and getting a good understanding of the impact of these issues on the business. The five stages are:

1. *Determine the key issues*: Work with the business to determine the issues of most concern, regardless of whether they have any obvious links to HR.
2. *Determine the impact on the business*: This entails digging deeper into the consequences of unresolved problems in the business. For example, what is the result of decisions being avoided?
3. *Develop collaborative solutions*: Working in Partnership with the client group to determine how HR can help.
4. *Establish measurable outcomes*: If the impact on the business is clear, then it should be possible to identify key business information that should be improved.
5. *Assess effectiveness*: This needs to be done on an ongoing basis, re-tuning and reshaping the problem as it emerges in partnership with the client group.

Boudreau and Ramstad (1997)

This model separates out the impact that HR practices have on the efficiency of internal processes from the impact on employee behaviours and strategic business results. The model is simple and has three levels of evaluation:

1. What HR does
2. What HR makes happen
3. Business success.

This has a lot of similarities to the Balanced Scorecard approach, highlighted earlier in this chapter. The model links measures through a cause-and-effect chain, which helps managers to understand how different measures are related and how they ultimately contribute to the business results.

Cabrera (2003)

Cabrera has built on the earlier model by Boudreau and Ramstad and has developed a framework for evaluation which classifies HR measures into five distinct types.

219

1. Traditional HR operational measures – efficiency, cost, ratios, speed of offer letters, hours of training per employee
2. Organisational capability measures, where HR should have impact for example, employee behaviours, skills and attitudes
3. Measures of the impact of HR practices on organisational capabilities
4. Measures of the impact of organisational capabilities on strategic business results
5. Direct measures of the impact of HR practices on strategic business results.

She stresses that any evaluation model must incorporate an assessment of the causal links between the different levels. More complex analysis in this field would require predictive validity or utility analysis techniques, normally beyond the scope of most HR functions. Many researchers in the HR field, however, are trying to establish causal links, and the recent work of Guest et al. (2000) is aimed at gaining a better understanding of how HR affects performance.

Summary

The evidence suggests that few Business Partnerships are engaged in comprehensive evaluation processes. However, Business Partners are under increasing pressure to show that they are adding value to the business. To do this they need to work effectively with their clients to determine the best way to help the organisation progress and to set in place appropriate measures of success. At the start of any project it is essential that the Business Partner and the client collaborate on the bottom-line measures. It is also likely that the impact of any Partnership will need to be measured in both quantitative and qualitative ways, in order to show a more enriched picture of the value being added.

Depending on the nature of the intervention being evaluated, existing HR and OD models may provide an appropriate framework for evaluation. However, to evaluate the Business Partnership Function as a whole, it is likely that the framework will need to draw on an initial understanding of the strategic aims and the contribution the Partner is seeking to make. The newly emerging Partnership models provide a good basis for this analysis.

The selection of a particular framework for evaluation is a complex one and does not have a simple answer. Effective evaluation is about thinking through the purposes of the intervention and its intended outcome on the business; the purposes of the evaluation and how the data will be used; the audiences for the results of the evaluation; the points at which measurements can be taken; the difficulties in accessing the necessary data; the time and resources available; and the overall framework which is to be utilised. Ideally, Business Partners should seek to conduct the most informative evaluation possible, given these differing needs and the constraints of each situation.

Checklist

- Are you clear on what you are trying to achieve?
- Have you established an adequate focus on evaluation up front?
- Have you involved your client in establishing a framework for evaluation?
- What does a successful evaluation look like to your client?
- Are the measures you have selected appropriate, given the timescales?
- Are the measures you have selected both accessible and relevant?
- Have you separated out validation of the process from evaluation of the impact?
- Are you committed to carrying out the evaluation?
- Are you clear on how you will use the evaluation data?
- Are there existing HR evaluation models which can be utilised?
- Is there a clear requirement for either hard or soft measures?
- What depth and level of analysis is appropriate, given the work being evaluated?
- What links can be drawn between the work being undertaken and the predicted impact on the business?

References

Abernathy, D. J. (1999) 'Thinking Outside the Evaluation Box', *Training and Development*, Vol. 53, No. 2, February, pp. 18–23.

Alliger, G. M. and Janak, E. A. (1989) 'Kirkpatrick's Levels of Training Criteria: Thirty Years Later', *Personnel Psychology*, Vol. 42, No. 2, pp. 331–342.

Becker, B. E. and Huselid, M. A. (1998) 'High Performance Work Systems and Firm Performance: A Synthesis of Research and Managerial Implications', in G. Ferris (ed.) *Research in Personnel and Human Resource Management*, Vol. 16, pp. 53–101.

Blanchard, P. N., Thacker, J. W. and Way, S. A. (2000), 'Training Evaluation: Perspectives and Evidence from Canada', *International Journal of Training and Development*, Vol. 4, No. 4, pp. 295–304.

Boudreau, J. and Ramstad, P. M. (1997) 'Measuring Intellectual Capital: Learning from Financial History', *Human Resource Management*, Vol. 36, No. 3, pp. 343–356.

Brocket, S. (2004) 'Becoming a Business Partner: HR at Coca-Cola Enterprises', *Strategic HR Review*, Vol. 3, No. 2, January/February.

Cabrera, E. F. (2003), 'Strategic Human Resource Evaluation', *Human Resource Planning*, Vol. 26, No. 1, pp. 41–50.

Guest, D., Michie, J., Sheehan, M. and Conway, N. (2000) 'Getting Inside the HRM – Performance Relationship', Paper Presented at the 60th Annual Meeting of the Academy of Management, Toronto.

Herring, K. (2001) 'HR Takes a Hands-on Approach to Business and Delivers Results', *Workforce*, October, Vol. 80, No. 10, pp. 42–48.

Industrial Society (2000) 'Managing Best Practice', *Training Evaluation*, Vol. 70, April.

Kaplan, R. S. and Norton, D. P. (1996) 'Using the Balanced Scorecard as a Strategic Management System', *Harvard Business Review*, January–February, pp. 75–85.

Kearns, P. (2001) 'The Bottom Line HR Function', Spiro, London.

Kearns, P. (2003) 'HR Strategy: Business Focused, Individually Centred', Butterworth-Heinemann.

Kearns, P. and Miller, T. (1997) 'Measuring the Impact of Training and Development on the Bottom Line', *FT Management Briefings*, Pitman Publishing, London.

Kirkpatrick, D. L. (1996) 'Great Ideas Revisited: Revisiting Kirkpatrick's Four-Level Model', *Training & Development*, Vol. 50, No. 1, January, pp. 54–57.

Ministry of Defence (2001) *Training and Evaluation Toolkit*, July.

Pfau, B. N. and Cundiff, B. B. (2002) '7 Steps Before Strategy', *Workforce*, Vol. 81, No. 12, November, pp. 40–44.

Pulley, M. L. (1994) 'Navigating the Evaluation Rapids', *Training and Development*, Vol. 48, No. 9, September, pp. 19–24.

Rough, J. (1994) 'Measuring Training From a New Science Perspective', *Journal for Quality and Participation*, Vol. 17, No. 6, pp. 12–16.

Tamkin, P., Yarnall, J. and Kerrin, M. (2002) 'Kirkpatrick and Beyond: A Review of Models of Training Evaluation', Institute of Employment Studies, Report 392.

Warr, P. B., Allan, C. and Birdi, K. (1999) 'Predicting Three Levels of Training Outcome', *Journal of Occupational and Organisational Psychology*, Vol. 72, pp. 351–375.

11

Conclusions

This final chapter of our book provides us with an opportunity to reflect back on some of our learning about the role of the Business Partner and consider how it is evolving in the reality of the different organisational contexts.

It is perhaps too easy to neatly summarise where the role of the Business Partner ought to be or how we think it should look in practice. We could, as we have in some of the other chapters, come up with a neat Business Partner 'to do' list – put into place these 10 steps for effective Business Partnership and all your challenges for providing a strategic service will be resolved.

However, we all know that in reality things are never quite that straightforward. How the Business Partner role needs to be in your organisation will depend on the market you are in, the services you provide, what your client's needs are and the resources available to you. The chapters in themselves provide a framework which is worth holding in mind for developing the Business Partner Function. If time and attention is paid to the purpose of setting up a strategic HR role, which sits alongside senior managers in the business, it is more likely that the function will be successful. Working through the checklists at the end of each chapter will also provide a useful basis for reviewing your effectiveness.

What we have tried to pull together here are some practical elements, as well as highlighting the less tangible aspects of the role. For us, building good relationships within the HR function as well as with your internal clients is an essential part of the success of the role. You also need to have the ability to develop managerial capacity in the organisation to deal with the business challenges and move forward in the right direction for the company, taking people with you. This requires caring, competent, connected and challenging Business Partners who can enable the organisation to see what is missing as well as what is enabling within the present culture. We have called this the 4C approach to Business Partnership.

The 4C Approach to Business Partnership

Caring

Caring means being attuned to the human aspects of the role: paying attention to process as well as content issues; understanding the human condition and how people might react in times of change; paying attention to your own needs and drivers as well as those of others. Caring also means paying attention to the little things – sitting down and having a cup of tea with someone, spending time on small talk as well as business-focused conversations.

Competent

Competent means making sure you have the necessary knowledge about the business and organisations more widely; the ability to look ahead and anticipate what the business might need for the future; committing to continuous professional development; getting skilled in the areas in which you have less competence; and using others both within the HR team and from outside the organisation, who can meet the needs more effectively.

Connected

Connected means developing excellent relationships with all your stakeholders; understanding their needs and goals; understanding the politics of the organisation and how to work with integrity within the system; and connected to issues of corporate social responsibility and what this might mean for your organisation. Above all, working to keep connected with your self.

Challenging

Challenging means constantly pushing the boundaries of possibility within the business; challenging people and processes to deliver added value to the organisation. This also means challenging yourselves on a daily basis, to ensure that the Partnership is focused on the right issues.

Business Partners need to be constantly questioning themselves to achieve the best. Listed below are some of the questions that can help to provide a focus for the work of Business Partners in your organisation:

- Why do we want to work with our internal clients in this way?
- What are the drivers for setting up an internal Business Partnership Function?
- What is in it for our internal clients?
- What are some of the options around structuring the function?
- How will that structure best suit our client's needs?
- What services will be needed?
- At what level?
- Who will our primary customers be?
- What are our options for resourcing the function?
- What existing skills and capabilities do we have?
- Where are the gaps?
- How can we attract the right people for the roles?
- What training and development might people need to equip them for the roles successfully?
- What will their continuing professional development look like?
- How can we develop their capacity to think strategically, get alongside our internal clients and provide a value-added service to the business?
- What differences will this mean for our clients?
- What skills and resources will our clients need if we are to make a successful transition into a more strategic role?
- How do we support our client's needs around operational issues as well as the more strategic goals?
- How do we market our services and clarify what role we are now taking on?
- How can we continually monitor our services at both content and process levels?
- Do we know what our clients think about the service now?
- How can we capture their needs for the short, medium and longer term?
- What measures do we need to put in place for evaluating the success of our service?

Lessons from Best Practice

In writing this book, we were initially seeking to find a model of Best Practice from the companies we spoke to and drew examples from. What became increasingly clear as the research progressed was that the wide variety of examples of Business Partnership in operation meant that the findings were too diverse and organisation-specific to make this possible. Even within one organisation, there were often examples of effective and less effective Business Partners, depending on the nature of the individual and the stage of development of the business unit.

So what conclusions can we draw from the case studies we uncovered? While this book and the examples we have used to illustrate the aspects of the Business Partner role will never apply wholesale to every organisation, what we think can be pulled together are some guiding principles for good practice. These guidelines and principles will then need to be interpreted and tailored to meet the needs of the specific organisational context.

Guiding Principles for the Business Partner Role

These principles encapsulate for us the essence of the Business Partner role.

- Clear purpose and strategic intent
- Working collaboratively with internal clients
- Helping to improve the business and quality of people's working lives
- Open to learning and sharing learning with others
- Adding value by clarifying what is needed and evaluating outcomes
- Working with integrity for the greater good
- Supporting each other as well as our internal clients
- Committed to continuous professional development.

Appendix

Self-Assessment Questionnaire

Guidelines for completion

Review the following list of skills and behaviours to identify your current performance as a Business Partner. Having completed the questionnaire, review the aspects you have rated as needing more attention and use this to focus on your key development needs.

Section 1: Delivering to the business

	I do this well	I need to do more of this	This is not relevant
Holistic overview			
1. I understand systems thinking and use this to consider the impact of interventions	☐	☐	☐
2. I understand the bigger organisational context and future vision and strategy of the company	☐	☐	☐
3. I demonstrate a good understanding of the business environment	☐	☐	☐
4. I encourage discussions which help identify things stopping the organisation from moving forward	☐	☐	☐
5. I am a strategic thinker – taking a helicopter view on business needs	☐	☐	☐

	I do this well	I need to do more of this	This is not relevant
Plays many roles successfully			
6. I am able to flex my skill and experience to suit a wide variety of business needs	☐	☐	☐
7. I am able to provide both expert advice and support and guidance appropriately	☐	☐	☐
8. I identify and use appropriate specialists where boundaries of the role end	☐	☐	☐
Long-term perspective			
9. I avoid getting bogged down in the operational side of HR work	☐	☐	☐
10. I delegate appropriately to others	☐	☐	☐
11. I keep up to date with trends inside and outside the sector which may have business implications	☐	☐	☐
12. I help to shape the direction of the business in line with strategic priorities	☐	☐	☐

My overall sense of my performance in Section 1:

_____

_____

_____

Section 2: Working alongside managers in the business

	I do this well	I need to do more of this	This is not relevant
Collaboration and empowerment			
1. I develop good internal networks across my defined area of the business	☐	☐	☐
2. I build and maintain effective relationships with people outside my functional area	☐	☐	☐
3. I engage relevant key stakeholders and sponsors	☐	☐	☐
4. I actively involve others in the decision-making process	☐	☐	☐
5. I ensure that clients are confident and competent to carry on after any intervention	☐	☐	☐
People-oriented			
6. I build strong relationships with clients quickly	☐	☐	☐
7. I am able to build and maintain rapport with a wide range of people	☐	☐	☐
8. I demonstrate empathy and understanding in challenging times	☐	☐	☐
9. I build trust by getting to know clients and their needs well	☐	☐	☐
10. I identify and work with the strengths of others in the team	☐	☐	☐
11. I share knowledge and information with others	☐	☐	☐
Towards 'win'			
12. I ensure that contracts are in place for specific areas of work which meet the needs of the client and the business	☐	☐	☐

	I do this well	I need to do more of this	This is not relevant
13. I monitor contracts at both the content and the process level	☐	☐	☐
14. I clarify the boundaries of both my role and the work to be carried out	☐	☐	☐
15. I avoid creating unrealistic expectations by my clients	☐	☐	☐
16. I act with political sensitivity towards 'win' situations for individuals and the business	☐	☐	☐

My overall sense of my performance in Section 2:

_____

_____

_____

Section 3: Self-awareness and impact

	I do this well	I need to do more of this	This is not relevant
Focused on learning			
1. I question basic assumptions about self and others in order to heighten learning	☐	☐	☐
2. I continually seek self-improvement	☐	☐	☐
3. I demonstrate a good awareness of strengths and areas for development	☐	☐	☐
4. I use learning as a basis for future development	☐	☐	☐
5. I seek opportunities to move out of my comfort zone	☐	☐	☐

	I do this well	I need to do more of this	This is not relevant
6. I share learning about the organisation and business issues with others	☐	☐	☐
7. I choose self-development opportunities which are appropriate to needs	☐	☐	☐
Self-expression			
8. I actively promote the business of the organisation through deeds and words	☐	☐	☐
9. I demonstrate credibility by understanding the business and the range of issues facing managers	☐	☐	☐
10. I am resilient – able to cope with the day-to-day pressures	☐	☐	☐
11. I am able to maintain an appropriate work–life balance	☐	☐	☐
12. I present information in a confident and clear way which meets the needs of the audience	☐	☐	☐
Dynamism			
13. I am regarded as someone who 'walks the talk'	☐	☐	☐
14. I act as a role model for others in the organisation	☐	☐	☐
15. I engage others by showing a real interest in them as individuals	☐	☐	☐
16. I am approachable and visible	☐	☐	☐
17. I bring visible energy and drive to the role	☐	☐	☐

My overall sense of my performance in Section 3:

_____

_____

_____

Section 4: Creating and leading change

	I do this well	I need to do more of this	This is not relevant
Proactive and preventive			
1. I am proactive in seeking opportunities within the business to support strategy	☐	☐	☐
2. I anticipate likely obstacles to implementing business change	☐	☐	☐
3. I apply knowledge and understanding of change theory to implement changes successfully	☐	☐	☐
4. I strike an appropriate balance between achieving the business goals and managing emotional reactions to change	☐	☐	☐
5. I use influence to engage others in the change process	☐	☐	☐
Innovation and entrepreneurship			
6. I find creative ways to work with managers, drawing on a range of methodologies to support business needs	☐	☐	☐
7. I am able to work independently and make strategic decisions aimed at business improvement	☐	☐	☐
8. I look for and identify solutions beyond the obvious	☐	☐	☐

	I do this well	I need to do more of this	This is not relevant
Pathfinding			
9. I am able to cope with ambiguity and complexity	☐	☐	☐
10. I work on the edge of my own comfort zones	☐	☐	☐
11. I identify new possibilities to take the business forward and create competitive advantage	☐	☐	☐

My overall sense of my performance in Section 4:

_____

_____

_____

Section 5: Maintaining a business focus

	I do this well	I need to do more of this	This is not relevant
Prioritising			
1. I place the right priority on business needs in the light of longer-term goals	☐	☐	☐
2. I recognise the need to withdraw from a piece of work and move on without impacting relationships	☐	☐	☐
3. I demonstrate an understanding of the difference between urgent and important	☐	☐	☐
4. I utilise business data to help shape the direction of the business	☐	☐	☐
5. I am able to challenge appropriately and say no when necessary	☐	☐	☐

	I do this well	I need to do more of this	This is not relevant
Utilising feedback			
6. I actively seek and review feedback as the basis for insight and learning	☐	☐	☐
7. I demonstrate learning from feedback by applying new ways of working	☐	☐	☐
8. I look for ways to improve the service of the Business Partner provision	☐	☐	☐
9. I seek to enhance relationships and actions by thorough questioning during reviews	☐	☐	☐
Demonstrating effectiveness			
10. I set appropriate measures at the start of any project	☐	☐	☐
11. I ensure buy-in from the business to the evaluation process	☐	☐	☐
12. I utilise evaluation data to demonstrate the added value of interventions and the impact on business strategy	☐	☐	☐

My overall sense of my performance in Section 5:

_____

_____

_____

Index